ASIAN GIRLS ARE GOING PLACES

Michelle Law

Illustrations by Joey Leung
Artwork by Louise Zhang

Hardie Grant

EXPLORE

Foreword

Hello. If you are reading this right now, you are either an Asian woman interested in travelling, an Asian woman's relative/friend/colleague who is trying to determine whether or not this book will make a worthwhile gift (it will – definitely buy it), or an older white gentleman interested in learning exactly which places Asian women are going to in order to procure one as a date to your adult daughter's wedding in an effort to enrage your ex-wife. If you are the latter, kindly close this book, cancel your forthcoming trip to Phuket, and promptly walk into the ocean. Farewell.

Everyone else: welcome! It's a pleasure to be spending time with you in the pages of this book, which for the longest time I struggled to write because it felt bizarre to be writing a travel guide in the midst of a global pandemic. Each time I tried writing, I'd find myself staring out the window forlornly, like a weatherbound Jane Austen character, except I was a Chinese Australian woman in lockdown wearing Hello Kitty pyjamas stained with chilli oil. How would a travel guide help when there was a deadly virus ravaging humanity, for which East Asians like myself were being blamed? When could we travel the world again? And how do you get chilli oil out of flannel? Thankfully, friends offered some perspective: 'Get people excited to travel again!'; 'You could help Asian women navigate a world where anti-Asian racism has increased due to the coronavirus'; and 'Michelle, writing a travel guide is a far more useful lockdown activity than eating cheese and singing *Hamilton* songs to your cat'. These felt like worthwhile reasons. So I dragged myself into the shower, changed into proper clothes, and got to work.

This book is about Asian women who are going places, by which I mean to say, it's a guide to navigating the world in your body, as an Asian woman. (To clarify: I use the term 'Asian' in this book to refer to South and East Asian women.) Asian women often aren't taken seriously; the stereotype is that we're demure, meek, submissive creatures who require protection and invite ownership. This generalisation is not only incorrect, it's also a public safety concern.

Because ... have you ever met an Asian woman? We are intimidating, astute, and contain a nuclear level of repressed rage. Think of your mothers, your grandmothers, your sisters, or any random Asian woman on the street. My cousin once told me about a mainland Chinese woman who took a shit on the floor of a Prada store – very defiantly – because the staff refused to let her use their bathroom. Fearless. This book is about that: reclaiming our place in the world, one metaphorical Prada floor at a time.

For the longest time, travel shows and guides have been the domain of white hosts and authors at varying stages of decomposition. How could they possibly offer specialised advice to anyone other than, well ... white men? Hence, this book. Granted, I'm just one, very specific kind of Asian woman (part of the Chinese diaspora, young, heterosexual, cisgender, able-bodied, and godless) and don't have all the answers. There are so many ethnicities, age groups, sexualities, abilities, and religions that exist under the umbrella term of 'Asian' that require and deserve speaking to, so I've worked hard to collate stories and advice from Asian women from many different backgrounds, from all around the world.

I hope this guide is relatable, accessible, and real. And I hope that it's a small antidote to the traditionally dry, exoticising, and Anglo-centric travel canon that leaves many readers feeling more lost than found. This book is dedicated to you: Asian women who have travelled, have dreams to travel, or are aching to travel again soon.

TRAVEL

OMPANIONS

You've booked the plane tickets. You've found accommodation. Now you've got to figure out who you'll be taking on your trip.

But who exactly makes the best travel companion? Is it your family? Your friends? Your romantic partner? Or should you say 'to hell with you all – I'm going it alone'? The correct answer is ... that there is no correct answer. (I'm lying – the best travel companion is obviously your dog or cat, but they aren't the most practical option, unfortunately.) But hopefully this chapter helps provide some clarity on who to travel with, and offers some insight into how to navigate (and hopefully nurture) interpersonal relationships on the road.

Family

Something my non-Asian friends don't understand is why I have travelled so much with my family. Ah, those sweet, innocent babes; if only they knew I simply had no choice.

Asians are, generally speaking, tight-knit and family focused; they're fiercely protective and governed by principles of filial piety, so wherever your family goes, you must go. Whatever your family eats, you must eat. Whatever your family does, you must do. As the youngest of five children, I spent my childhood drooling on my sister's shoulder on Greyhound buses, on long-haul flights using my mum's lap as a pillow, or strapped into our family's eight-seater van en route to theme parks and wildlife sanctuaries on the weekends.

Now that I'm an adult, I've continued travelling with family because I genuinely enjoy it. I trust my family unequivocally and so they make fantastic travel companions: they know that I get motion sickness and are happy to stop during long car rides so I can spew on the roadside; I know that they'll be carrying snacks when I'm hungry because we're all prone to becoming hangry (hungry-angry); and they've seen me wee in the bushes. Multiple times. Despite my parents being divorced and my siblings and I being very different people, we all get along remarkably well.

In this chapter, you'll find the answers to questions like 'What are some fun activities to do with family members of all ages, from children to elderly parents?'; 'Do I need to enforce a bed time for my parents when we're travelling?' (Yes, a couple of hours after dinner); and 'How many adult children does it take to wrangle a parent out of an adult store in Japan after they've been scolded by the staff for taking photographs of sex toys?' (Three).

How to have a successful family trip

Choose your destination

Choose a family-friendly destination suitable for five adult children and their mother, who is in her sixties. Say, New Zealand. Ignore the fact that the last trip you took as a group was over twenty years ago and culminated in your parents separating and ultimately divorcing. Everything is going to be fine!

Get on the plane

Arrive at the airport five hours early at a designated meeting point. Do not, I repeat, do not waste four hours catching up, leaving only half an hour until boarding time, at a gate that is a ten-minute walk away from where security checks are occurring. Because the first thing that will happen is your mother, the aforementioned woman in her sixties, WILL test positive for explosives and WILL need to spend ten minutes emptying her enormous handbag for airport security to inspect. Do not rush the airport security guard by exclaiming, 'ALL SHE HAS IN THERE IS A FLASK FULL OF HOT WATER, A SOFT PACK OF TISSUES, AND EVERY CLINIQUE TRAVEL MINI EVER MANUFACTURED, LET THE WOMAN GO!' Avoid losing your cool, because the security guard is already deeply suspicious of this Chinese woman in a big floppy hat and sunglasses, both of which she must wear indoors to protect her glaucoma-affected, light-sensitive eyes. (Upon reflection, this physical description does make my mother sound like a terrorist.) Once your mother has received the all clear, sprint to the gate while screaming your collective fury at the ineptitude of the security guard, who was reading false positives because he'd forgotten to change the swab on his testing wand. Find your seats on the already seated plane, catch your breath, and then stress eat from an enormous sack of candy packed by your eldest brother.

Revert to your childhood self

Accept that when you are in the presence of your family, regardless of how old you may be, you will revert to the same roles you had as children, thereby shedding the identity you have crafted for yourself over the course of your adult life. What's that? You're a successful lawyer? Who cares – you vomited on Space Mountain at Disneyland. You're a trained ICU nurse? What does that matter if you couldn't swim to the opposite side of the lake during school holidays because you're afraid of deep water? You're a loving and devoted stay-at-home parent? No one cares because remember that time you couldn't get past Bowser's castle in Super Mario and threw the Nintendo 64 out the window in a rage? On family holidays, the established hierarchy reigns supreme. This is how you end up sleeping in a foldable cot in the middle of the hallway, because you are the youngest child. Your eldest sister and brother have first dibs on the bedrooms, but they will also organise the rental car as the three younger children run amok outside with your mother, taking silly photos.

Have a surprisingly good time

You may be anticipating a family fight at some point, over the TV remote, or sharing food, or the fact someone has used all of the hot water, leaving the rest of you to hastily splash cold water over your armpits and privates. But surprisingly, this blowup may not ever happen. Perhaps you've spent enough of your childhoods arguing and now you're all old enough to know when to pick your battles. Instead, you'll spend the days stopping by roadsides in Auckland, with the backdrop of magnificent, endless mountain ranges stretched across the horizon, and walking down to untouched beaches. You'll edge your way down to the shore, two of you guiding your mother across the rocks, until you reach some shallow rock pools where some seals and their pups are lounging during the low tide. The seals will gaze at you, wide eyed, and occasionally yawn – these lazy, sleepy sea dogs. Another day, a thick mist will hover in the air, light rain slowly saturating the outer layers of your clothes. You'll take a long car ride up a mountain to a chairlift that transports you through the mist and over the treetops, all of you screaming with exhilaration as your legs dangle into nothingness at the edge of a cliff face.

Push your luck

Things may be going so wonderfully that you decide a guided kayak tour is a great activity in which to involve your mother, despite the fact that she cannot swim. Yes, a woman who engages in very little physical activity (and who, one year, demanded that you return the adult swimming lessons you bought her for Christmas) should absolutely be taken into the open ocean! And yet, for some unknown reason, your mother agrees to the tour. And somehow, even with the rolling, chopping waves that cause your mother to squeal with excitement and fear, the kayaking is a roaring success. Everyone is so delirious at pulling off this family activity that it takes until the evening for you to notice that you are all horribly seasick, and spend the rest of the night clutching walls, bedside tables, and the backs of chairs to prevent you throwing up or collapsing from dizziness, or both. For a family trip to go this smoothly, there had to be a catch.

On the road again, or, the tale of being trapped in a seven-hour traffic jam.

4pm My mother, older brother, older sister and I start making our way back to Brisbane, the capital city of Queensland, in Australia, after a day trip on the Sunshine Coast visiting family. From where we are, the trip normally takes ninety minutes without traffic. We're in the family hatchback, the windows of which are being flecked with light rain. It's a sun shower.

4.20pm Traffic slows to a crawl as the rain intensifies; it isn't heavy, but it's persistent. We turn on the radio to see if there's been an accident ahead, but there are no traffic reports. We're also out of range of reception so our phones are of no use.

4.40pm Traffic grinds to a complete halt. People are starting to turn off their engines and hopping out of their cars, hands up to their eyes to block out the rain and the glare of the setting sun. They're trying to see what is holding up the traffic ahead, but all that's visible is kilometres of cars stretching either way on the highway. We are surrounded by logging forestry – some kind of pine trees planted in perfect, eerie rows – and billboards advertising strawberry picking and cures for erectile dysfunction.

5pm   People are leaving their cars to stretch their legs and pee in the bushes. It's still raining. We check the radio again – still no news – and finally decide to turn off our engine too.

5.30pm   We need to pee. Outside, the rain continues to fall steadily. My mother, my sister and I squat on the roadside and try to cover our bare butts as best we can with umbrellas. It's getting dark.

6.30pm   It's evening. We've spent the last hour scanning the radio and again, there are no reports. If it was an accident, why haven't any ambulances or emergency services come? We joke that maybe it's the end of the world and the people on this highway are the last living humans on earth.

7pm   People have set up shanty towns on the highway, pulling out camping chairs and playing cards, smoking and drinking in the back of their pickup trucks. Others are taking their children and dogs for walks up and down the length of the highway, to ease their boredom. We take stock of all the food we have in the car in case we need to spend the night on the highway. We have water, some candy, some mints, and a muesli bar. We pass the time by debating who in the car we will eat first if worst comes to worst.

8.30pm   My brother goes out to pee and afterwards we take shifts sleeping in case the traffic decides to move. The rain starts to ease.

10pm   The traffic hasn't budged for hours. Are we going to die here?! But at least the rain has stopped.

11pm   Up ahead, there is movement ... people are returning to their cars. Along the stretch of highway, others are catching on – it's like a Mexican wave of excitement as engines roar to life. We drive until we discover what was causing the jam: a bridge had flooded and emergency services had been spending all evening creating an alternate route for drivers. It wasn't the end of the world and we didn't even need to resort to cannibalism! We scream and cheer, delirious with fatigue, right until we get home. None of us want to be in a car ever again.

We joke that maybe it's the end of the world and the people on this highway are the last living humans on earth.

ASIAN GIRLS ARE GOING PLACES

Christmas in Canada

If Hollywood is anything to go by, grandmothers are supposed to be sweet, grey-haired little ladies who enjoy knitting and pulling their grandchildren into warm embraces as the smell of freshly baked choc chip cookies wafts from an oven.

The grandmother I grew up with – my Ma Ma – lived with my father in the next suburb over after my parents split up. She was a hardy, pragmatic woman with a dirty sense of humour who loved mah jong, burping loudly after drinking beers, growing melons, force-feeding us, and power walking around the neighbourhood in bargain bin sneakers she found at the department store. (She is one of the most badass women I have ever known and I'm honoured to be her granddaughter.) And while I loved my Ma Ma, I wondered if my Por Por, far away in Canada, might be different.

I'd only met my Por Por once, when I was four, and I remembered her cracking jokes and having a croaky, low voice; the rest I was left to imagine for myself. When I was eleven, my mum told me that she and I would be travelling to Canada to visit Por Por, now in her late seventies, and so I began obsessing about the kind of relationship we might have. 'Can you love a stranger?' I'd ask my mum as we prepped for the trip. 'Because I feel like I love Por Por already and so much I could burst!' Once we arrived in Toronto, I was much more reserved, shy around this matriarch whose language I couldn't speak, and who had so many grandchildren I wondered how she might possibly be interested in getting to know one more. Beyond that, I wasn't feeling like myself. I was moody, often for no reason, and I felt incredibly lonely being away from my siblings. While I was stuck in the dead of winter in a foreign country, they were together in sunny Australia, eating ice blocks and going to the beach.

I wanted nothing more than to leave Canada, and so I withdrew into myself, threw tantrums, played computer games for hours on end, gave my mum and Por Por the silent treatment, and felt inexplicably lethargic no matter how much I slept. (I didn't know this at the time but I was about to get my period for the first time ever.)

Things were not going as I'd imagined: where I wanted embraces and the kind of kinship my friends had with their non-Asian grandmothers, I found awkwardness and an inability to communicate (my Por Por couldn't speak English and I speak broken Cantonese). I resented my Por Por and ate the dinners she lovingly prepared for us in silence. I would leave mealtimes angry, and then feel deeply contrite. 'I feel bad for being mean to Por Por,' I tearily confessed to my mum one evening as we drifted to sleep. 'It's okay,' she cooed. 'Por Por had seven children. Por Por understands.'

We decided to extend our trip and spend Christmas in Canada, which was being hosted by my adult cousin, his wife and their young children. Throughout the day, I was on the verge of tears as my cousin's kids tore open their presents. I had never spent Christmas away from home, and gift-giving is our family's way of showing love, that we know each other intimately enough to make or purchase meaningful presents that the other person can treasure. The one gift I received was a surprise, from one of my cousin's wife's relatives, and when I opened it I was puzzled: it was a gaudy brooch in the shape of an owl, its ruby red eyes staring threateningly at me from the box. I was touched by the gesture, but also gutted – the brooch was clearly a regift, made obvious by the fact it was an accessory more suited to a pensioner than an eleven-year-old child.

I spent the rest of the day moping around the house by myself, with all the moodiness of a kid on the precipice of becoming a teenager. Later in the afternoon, my Por Por waved me over to where she'd been sitting quietly in a corner of the living room. 'Mun Yee, this is for you.' She handed me a lai see (red envelope with money inside) and patted my hand softly. In that moment I understood that despite her countless grandchildren and great-grandchildren, and despite the fact we knew so little of each other, I was important to her. She loved me, and was expressing that love her own way, in a way that she was comfortable with. It was a surprising and moving gesture, and better than any kind of false expectation I'd created for myself. Now, almost twenty years later, my Por Por has since passed away. I still have the lai see that she gifted me.

Family-friendly destinations for all ages

Italy

Florence is a wonderful city for families as it's slightly slower paced than Rome and Venice. The architecture and public gardens (head to the quieter Renaissance garden, Giardino Bardini, rather than the crowded Boboli Gardens) are oh-so-charming, and there is a gelato flavour out there to please even the fussiest family member. The Ponte Vecchio is a particularly beautiful spot at which to stop and take stock before exploring the shops lining its walkway.

Spain

Spain in the summertime feels like a dream: it's relaxed, sleepy and the perfect weather to dine al fresco over shared plates. The Museo Nacional del Prado is a must-see; it houses some of the world's most famous artworks, including some by Rembrandt and Bosch among many others. And make time to explore more than one of Gaudi's buildings, which will inspire awe and joy in the young, old, and everyone in between.

New Zealand

If you're looking for something slower in pace, New Zealand is a stunning country with a rich cultural history in which you can reset. Not to mention the natural environment is so jaw-droppingly beautiful that each morning you'll wake up believing you've stumbled right into a postcard. Take some nature walks and meet a kakapo or kiwi, have a spa day at a geothermal pool like Hell's Gate, or nerd out and explore a Hobbit house.

Japan

Japan is the perfect destination if you have never travelled with family before as it's accessible, affordable and safe. If you're after a slower and more mindful activity check out Kinkaku-ji, the Hiroshima Peace Memorial Museum or Japan's art island, Naoshima. And if you're after something a touch more thrilling, visit the Osaka aquarium or Tokyo DisneySea, or marvel at the wild deer at Miyajima Island.

Costa Rica

For those nature-loving families. Relax on Costa Rica's pristine beaches or explore its national parks: Manuel Antonio National Park is a sure-fire hit and is bursting with local fauna. Then check out the numerous wildlife sanctuaries and nature reserves aimed at educating visitors about the importance of preserving natural ecosystems. The adults can enjoy coffee plantation tours (and tastings, of course).

Indonesia

If you're after a true 'holiday' in every sense of the word – rest, relaxation, and restoration – you can't go past the town of Ubud. Take the family on an adventure to the Ubud Art Market or the Sacred Monkey Forest Sanctuary. Do a bike tour through rice fields. Take a cooking class together. Or get a massage in town, or at one of the many hotels nestled in dense, tropical forest.

Family-friendly activities

1

Revive old family rivalries with board games, card games, ten-pin bowling or laser tag.

2

Go to a shopping centre. You don't need to buy anything; shopping centres are a convenient pit stop for food, bathrooms, and rest.

3

Do a cook-up together. Or spend time learning recipes from your elders. Video tape them making your favourite meals and record their voices because, as morbid as it sounds, they won't be with you forever and the recipes for your favourite meals and snacks will one day be lost with them.

4

Go to the casino ... for the buffet. Afterwards, the grandparents can enjoy some light gambling while the kids can be taken to see a show. (Side note: if you're in a larger group, split up according to which activity each person wants to do to ensure everyone stays happy and complaint free.)

5

For the adults only – go on a wine tour or visit a brewery. Getting tipsy with your family members and seeing them on a very human level can be an icebreaker during awkward trips. (I can neither confirm nor deny that seeing my grandparents/parents several drinks deep has led to the unearthing of family secrets that have been profusely denied in the stark light of day.)

6

When you're sick of speaking to each other, have a movie night with lots of snacks.

7

Do some low-intensity sports together, like swimming, table tennis, or badminton.

8

Take group photos. It's not often families are all together: people get married and start their own families; kids start going to school; and older folks pass away. Value your trip together, even during the stressful times.

9

Go camping! Fork out for a camping site that has hot showers and electricity, and spend some time catching up around the fire eating toasted marshmallows.

Top tips!

- Explore your own backyard and choose a travel destination that's closer to home. This is a more budget-friendly option, is easier to organise, and gives everyone peace of mind in case of an emergency.

- If you're driving, take a lot of pit stops for everyone to get out and stretch their legs.

- Pack a lot of snacks so people can graze over the course of the day.

- Allow yourselves lots of time and don't make your day jam-packed; rather, have a wish list of activities and a loose daily schedule. This way you won't be thrown by inevitable delays.

- Bring a polaroid camera. In the age of smart phones, having a physical token from your trip as a family feels more special.

- Have a designated meeting spot each time your group splits up.

- Travel insurance, travel insurance, travel insurance. Buy it early for a discounted rate, and in the event you have to cancel the trip.

- Pack as light as possible.

- If you're travelling with older folks who are able-bodied, exercise with them before the trip. This way, they'll feel well supported and stronger in their own bodies in order to undertake light to medium walking.

When sleeping women wake, mountains move

Chinese proverb

Travelling solo

One of life's greatest pleasures is to be alone. Anyone who believes it's embarrassing or pathetic to travel solo clearly doesn't understand that there is a difference between 'aloneness' and 'loneliness'. Loneliness is heartbreaking, but aloneness? It's empowering, freeing. Travelling alone means that you have no one to answer to and no one for whom you are responsible. The only person you have to worry about is yourself, and you can do whatever you please: burp in restaurants, people-watch for hours, grow out your body hair, fart in the hotel bath, or buy half a dozen velvet cupcakes from Magnolia Bakery in New York and devour them all while watching *Say Yes to the Dress* on TLC. (I may or may not have done all of these things.)

An older woman I know once said to me, 'Relish the periods of your life when you are single, because once you meet someone or have kids, you'll never be alone again for the rest of your life.' That woman was my mother: she had five children and an unhappy marriage to my father. Now she's in her sixties and refuses to date anyone because she 'spent most of her adult life wiping poo off babies and I don't want to spend the rest of my life nursing an incontinent old man'. She gives excellent advice, and I repeat it to myself every day.

Grieving at the Great Barrier Reef

More people should be tourists in their home countries; it's so easy to settle into the humdrum of daily life and forget the riches around you.

I was born and grew up in Australia and my entire life I'd never been to the Great Barrier Reef, which has been steadily heating to death at a rapid rate due to climate change. With this in mind, I set aside a few weeks in my schedule to travel to an eco-resort on Lady Elliot Island, the southernmost coral cay of the reef and an area with very minor coral bleaching. In hindsight, I made this trip for somewhat morbid reasons: I wanted to be alone to purge myself of a failed relationship with a man I believed was my forever person, and I wanted to say goodbye to the reef before it was too late. (What did I say? Morbid.) One of my sisters offered to accompany me, knowing that I was in the early stages of grieving, but I was confident in my decision to travel alone; it would be empowering and rejuvenating returning to myself, snorkelling with sea turtles and manta rays and growing fat on the daily lunch and dinner buffets included in my trip package.

However, when I boarded the seaplane it became apparent that I was headed to a destination that primarily catered for families and couples; you either went there to procreate or spend time with your offspring, not to wander the shores like a grieving spectre. They were also all white and didn't know what to make of a bald (I have alopecia, which is an autoimmune disease that causes baldness) young, Asian woman smiling benignly from the back seats of the plane. If the island lost power and all connection to the outside world would I become the Piggy to their Roger? The other passengers – a family of four, and a friendly couple – smiled at me pityingly, as I tried ignoring my impending sense of doom. However these feelings were only compounded when I arrived at the resort to discover they had upgraded me to a family apartment, which would have been incredible under any other circumstance, except in this circumstance I wanted to feel cocooned and safe, not thrown into a four-bedroom-sized abyss.

The fifty or so other people on the island soon caught on to the fact I was there alone. Halfway into my stay, the friendly couple from the plane adopted me and forced me to eat dinner with them. One evening, a resort staff member approached me as I was eating dinner to loudly exclaim, 'Hi! I notice that you are ALONE. Is everything okay here? Because you're ALONE, eating dinner ALL BY YOURSELF.' Everyone assumed that because I was a single woman holidaying by myself I must be mentally unwell, when in fact I was perfectly content. Each day I was swimming, exploring rock pools, going on nature walks, and having profound moments of catharsis I wouldn't have been able to experience with company.

My favourite moment of the trip was when, on a particularly still night, I took a blanket onto the beach and sat under the glowing stars. It was so dark I had to move slowly across the sand, guided only by the moonlight. Listening to the waves gently lapping the shore, I wrapped myself up and had a quiet cry, peering up in awe at these exploding balls of gas that had witnessed generations of heartbreak, and feeling thankful that I had the privilege to be alive and find love again one day.

There's really no such thing as the 'voiceless'. There are only the deliberately silenced, or the preferably unheard.

Arundhati Roy, Indian author

Swimming with the fishes

One of my favourite travel memories is snorkelling for the first time at the Phi Phi Islands in Thailand. As a keen fish hobbyist (yes, I am aware that I sound like the world's biggest nerd right now), swimming in the open seas surrounded by tropical fish is my idea of heaven.

But leading up to the snorkelling trip, I was extremely anxious about being bald in public. I've had alopecia since I was twelve; it's an autoimmune condition that causes hair loss, and over the years I've gone through periods of losing all my hair, only to have it grow back entirely, before losing it all again completely.

I'm lucky in the scheme of things – alopecia is a physically harmless disease (the hair loss itself isn't painful) – but the psychological fallout is immense, particularly as a young woman who is already made to feel self-conscious about every other aspect of her physical appearance. Normally, I wear a wig, but wearing a wig becomes impractical when you're dealing with water. For days, I wrestled with the idea of simply not going snorkelling – what was the point of going if I'd spend the entire time worrying about how I looked? But eventually, my desire to see those fish ultimately overrode my misgivings about my body. I steeled myself and booked the tour tickets.

On the boat to the island, there was one family – an older mother and father with a teenage daughter – who would not stop staring at me. It didn't matter that we were sailing past some of the most beautiful scenery on earth: crystalline water, limestone rocks rising majestically from the ocean, clear blue skies ... their gaze remained on me. I tried being the bigger person and smiled back at them, hoping this would make me appear less alien, but their expressions remained unchanged. As I removed my hat in order to attach my snorkelling gear, their eyes widened. In the water, as I hand-fed sliced banana to schools of tropical fish, they gawked at me through their foggy goggles. I felt like a zoo animal, more a part of the tour itself than a human being. I wished I could sink to the bottom of the ocean. Back on the boat, as we sped back to the mainland, they continued to stare at me until finally, I decided to stare back. I stared so hard that they became uncomfortable, until they broke their gaze and began focusing on the passing scenery. When their eyes flickered back to me – this stony, wet woman with droplets of water falling off her shiny, bare scalp – I stood my ground. By the time we returned to the mainland, they scuttled back into their tour bus without a backwards glance. It reminded me of a practice I sometimes like to adopt when I'm walking on a busy pathway: if a man is walking in the opposite direction to me, I do not make way for him. (Try it sometime and see what happens; I can guarantee there will be some collisions and bewilderment on the man's part.)

I still think of that family whenever I feel nervous about leaving the house without a wig on, but it's a lesson to myself to be unapologetic about illness and health aids. How other people react to you has nothing to do with you, and you are not the problem. Never feel ashamed of how you take up space in the world, because you deserve to live your life to the best of your ability, without regrets. Refuse to be small; refuse to take a back seat. If I hadn't chosen to go snorkelling, I would have missed out on one of the most elating experiences of my life.

Searching for home

In my early twenties, I decided I wanted to travel by myself for the first time with intentions to 'find myself' (cue eye roll), both as a young woman in the world and as someone who was born in and raised in a country that wasn't my ancestral homeland.

Both sides of my family are from the Guangdong province in Southern China and have since migrated all over the world. My parents moved to Australia from Hong Kong, so I regard it as my other home. I still remember the moment being an Asian person in an Asian country clicked for me: I was twelve years old and standing in the middle of a bustling intersection in Mong Kok and was so relieved to be invisible for the first time in my life. (Well, as long as I kept my mouth shut and didn't butcher Cantonese with my Australian accent!)

And so I had the idea that I might move to Hong Kong – to become closer to the Chinese parts of myself, to get to know my extended family, and to finally become fluent in Cantonese. I'd travelled to Hong Kong numerous times with my immediate family, and was always known as the 'baby', constantly having anecdotes of things I did as a child ('You loved to eat this particular brand of seaweed crackers!'; 'Remember that time you got lost at the Big Buddha and almost gave your mother a heart attack?') thrust upon me by my extended family. Now they were going to get to know me as a grown woman. I spent my time there eating yum cha with my aunt, playing badminton with my uncle and getting to know his new wife, helping with furniture shopping, babysitting the younger generations, and spending weekends drinking milk teas and going shopping with my cousins. But it didn't take long before I started to yearn for my other home, the one in which I'd grown up. I was at the mercy of that constant state of displacement experienced by diaspora kids.

I didn't end up moving to Hong Kong; the idea was exciting in theory, but in reality I was scared and unwilling to move away from my immediate family and everything I'd ever known. But the moment I left, I missed my extended family; I'd just started piecing together those parts of myself that had been fractured by migration, and now I was choosing to break myself apart again. But in many ways it is comforting knowing that I have connection points around the world upon whom I can depend, and vice versa. Yes, we are physically disconnected but we are bound by love, by blood, and by history. (And, of course, WhatsApp.)

I'm more observant when I travel on my own. When you travel with companions you wind up splitting your attention between the place you're in and the companion you're with. Of course that can be a worthy sacrifice, depending on your companion. But I've found that if you truly want to get to know a place it is better to go alone so that you are fully attuned to your surroundings and offering up your entire being.

Monica, Australia

Interview
with
Tammy Law

Tammy Law is a photographer
who is passionate about exploring
everyday stories that often
get overlooked. Informed by
her experiences of being Asian
Australian, Tammy's practice
explores the complexities of
displacement and the emotional,
psychological and physical
dislocations that occur.
(Full disclosure: she is also
the author's sister!)

ML   **What is your cultural background and how does it influence the way you move in the world?**

TL   My mum was born in Malaysia and grew up in Hong Kong, before moving to Australia. My dad was born in the south of China and lived in Hong Kong before moving to Australia. Being an Australian-born Chinese person influences the way in which I experience the world, the way I choose to travel in terms of places, and also how I conduct myself in different ways while in those places. My parents instilled in me the importance of education, so, being the good Chinese daughter that I am, I decided to take off after I had finished my undergraduate studies. For my first solo trip abroad I chose to travel to Japan and China. Japan was first on the list because I had a feeling that Japan would be a good country to ease me into the world of solo travel. I also was acutely aware that China would be a bit more brutal to navigate. The harshness of the mainland Chinese towards an Australian-Chinese 'alien' was enough to make me question this as a first stop – especially having travelled to Hong Kong numerous times and having a keen sense of awareness about how Chinese people living in Hong Kong and China perceive Chinese people living in Western countries (i.e., as privileged scum) and they're probably not wrong. I felt that these were destinations that were quite disparate but embodied different aspects of my identity. For instance, I'm quite a passive person and I think that passivity lends itself quite well when travelling through Japan because I felt like women in Japan are expected to fit a certain mould. I find that in Australia people who don't know me very well have this perception that I am quite mild-mannered, but in Japan I didn't feel like that quality made me stand out. In China I felt like it was more cut-throat, which reminded me of my grandmother and her brazen kind of attitude to life. Simple things (in Australia) like getting on a bus or asking for directions in China were terrifying tasks to me, where I felt like I had to prepare myself for a fight. These cultural negotiations made me reflect on how things come so easy to us in Australia and how survival has really been at the heart of our ancestors' journeys.

ML　　What countries have you travelled to alone and what did you do there?

TL　　As a freelance documentary photographer, my projects have taken me to many countries and most of them I have travelled to alone.

Burma (Myanmar) – Photographic projects and visiting friends.

Japan and China – I chose to travel for one year and ended up applying for a working holiday visa in Japan. I spent six months there and then travelled to China to learn more about my parents and ancestors, and the culture that we weren't immersed in as kids.

Inner Mongolia – Photographic projects and adventure.

Ethiopia – Photographic projects.

United Arab Emirates – Stopover and adventure.

ML   When did you start travelling alone and what do you love and dislike about it?

TL   I started travelling alone when I was twenty-one. I love the sense of quietness and the ability to be alone and comfortable. I also like the freedom/selfishness of being able to take risks and go on adventures without having to consult others. The kinds of people that I met along the way and the types of adventures that I went on, I think were largely due to the fact that I was travelling alone. It's hard being a single, Asian woman travelling solo though. There are countries that I will omit from my list of preferences when thinking about a solo trip, mainly because of safety reasons.

ML When you're travelling, what are people's reactions to seeing/meeting you: an Asian woman by herself?

TL I think while on my travels I try to align myself with people who live similarly to myself or share the same principles, so the expected reactions of people seeing/meeting me on my own were kind of nullified. However, this perception that women who travel on their own are adventurous and live lives that are out of the ordinary makes me slightly uncomfortable. I feel that if I were doing the things I do as a man, people wouldn't draw the same conclusions. Now as a mother, I feel as though people might label me as irresponsible or perceive me as someone who doesn't care for her family if I go away on my own.

... this perception that women who travel on their own are adventurous and live lives that are out of the ordinary makes me slightly uncomfortable. I feel that if I were doing the things I do as a man, people wouldn't draw the same conclusions.

ASIAN GIRLS ARE GOING PLACES

ML   **What is unique to the experience of travelling alone as an Asian woman?**

TL   You can definitely play the 'dumb young woman' card. For instance, if I am on assignment and I am on my own in a prohibited location, authorities seem less worried about my presence. When I was working on assignment along the Thai–Burma (Myanmar) border, the military from both sides were less likely to target me or see me as a threat because I looked the part.

ML   **How do you prepare for a solo trip – physically and mentally?**

TL   Physically, I might just aim to pack less because I only have myself to rely on. Mentally, I don't know if I make any conscious efforts to prepare myself, but I do know that I am on higher alert when walking alone after sunset, sleeping alone in a rental apartment, etc. I am more conscious of the fact that there is more to lose.

ML   **Does travelling solo help you grow as a person?**

TL   It absolutely helped me. I was a really anxious child and my first trip abroad by myself was a really significant journey that I think I needed to take in order for me to be able to position myself in the world and understand who and what matters to me.

ML   **How do you make friends or connections when you are travelling alone?**

TL   Hostels. I only felt comfortable meeting people in Japanese hostels though. There seems to be a different kind of community that gravitate towards hostels in Japan versus hostels in other countries.

Staying with host families. I stayed with host families in Japan and am still in touch with some of the families that I stayed with while living there.

Online. We're super lucky now that there are so many online platforms that enable people to meet others while travelling.

A couple of online platforms that I have used:

couchsurfing.com – An online platform to make friends and/or touch base with people who have a spare space or room to accommodate you for one or two nights – usually local people are hosts. This platform is now a paid service for extra protection for its users.

Language exchanges – I used these in Japan and China a lot to try to learn the language while travelling there, but also to meet locals and experience life from their perspectives. Just search for 'language exchanges' to find a platform that suits you.

ML What has been the most profound moment you've experienced while travelling alone that you wouldn't have been able to experience with company?

TL I think that travelling to a more dishevelled (and off the beaten track) part of the Great Wall of China was definitely something that came about through the fact that I was travelling on my own. I was couch surfing at the time and two of the other couch surfers who I met in Beijing were from Montreal and super lovely guys who I felt I could trust almost immediately – no seediness, just two friendly, genuine dudes (SUPER RARE). With our very basic, almost non-existent Mandarin, we hopped in a taxi and used a guidebook to navigate to what felt like the most unknown and undervalued part of The Great Wall.

When we arrived our taxi driver walked us through to the side of the wall where apple trees were planted. He disappeared for a moment and after speaking to the local who owned the land, he picked a couple of apples off the tree, washed them in a nearby natural spring and offered them to us. It felt a bit like the scene in Snow White where the witch offers Snow White a poisonous apple but we accepted and I still remember vividly just how crunchy and sweet that apple tasted. We asked him to stay while we climbed that section of the wall and offered to tip him handsomely, so he obliged. Some parts of that section of the wall were so unkempt that we climbed up parts of it on our hands and knees. When we got to the top it was the most stunning view of The Great Wall and surrounds. I remember that it was a crisp autumn day so the air had a bit of a cold bite but the sky was sunny and then the most profound thing happened – Dad called me! To get a call from him at that moment in our ancestral homelands felt incredible.

ML   **When I think of the adventures you've had, I'm reminded of a quote by designer Rei Kawakubo: 'My energy comes from freedom and a rebellious spirit.' You've always had that energy, from when you were a teenager, going on solo bike rides (and later motorbike rides). What drives your sense of adventure?**

TL   That's a great quote! Not sure if I'm rebellious but I definitely crave freedom and I think in many ways that desire to be independent and explore things outside of the life that we know has driven me and still drives me. I think curiosity is a thing that our parents nurtured and I think it's something that can easily get squashed during people's formative years. Being curious is something that I hope to nurture in [my son] Coen.

If one man can destroy everything, why can't one girl change it?

Malala Yousafzai,
Pakistani activist

MEMORABLE

Problem solving
MONICA, AUSTRALIA

Wearing all my clothes so that I could comply with the budget airline weight restrictions. I'm talking wearing multiple pairs of shoes here.

Sugar rush
TAMMY, AUSTRALIA

I think I drank the most soft drink that I have ever drunk while I travelled through Ethiopia because soft drink is often more common than water in really remote communities there.

ASIAN GIRLS ARE GOING PLACES

MOMENTS

Pitching in

GRACE, JAPAN

I volunteered after the big 2011 Tōhoku earthquake and tsunami and saw how communities work together to support each other in tragic times.

Sacred site

MONICA, AUSTRALIA

Uluru is truly astounding. Imagine driving through hundreds of kilometres of flat, semi-arid desert, and then out of nowhere rises a ginormous ochre-coloured loaf from the ground. No trees grow on it and the rock is smooth with lovely waved lines as if it has been sculpted by the hand of God. Unsurprisingly sections of the rock have deep spiritual significance for the Anangu people. It is astoundingly large, taking hours to walk around. The changing light gives it a different look and personality throughout the day.

Solo activities

1

Visit a local cinema.
(Make sure the film is subtitled
if you're in a country where
you don't speak the language!)

2

Do a cooking class
and learn how to prepare
a traditional meal.

3

Go for a walk or jog, or
hire a bike or scooter to
discover what's nearby your
accommodation for future
reference. Look out for
essentials like grocery stores,
cafes, pharmacies and parks.

4

Join a guided tour at a museum
or gallery.

5

Write and send postcards to loved ones.

6

Do some journalling.

7

Splurge at a deli or bakery and take yourself out on a picnic.

8

Find an independent bookstore. They will often have a cafe tucked away in the back or upstairs, which are lovely places to recharge with tea and cake. Many independent bookstores also have a list of upcoming events like book launches and author talks you can attend for free or for a small fee.

9

Go to a gig and discover some local musicians, artists or stand-up comedians.

10

Slow down and get a massage. You are allowed to relax and don't need to be moving at all times.

11

Take photos of yourself or ask others to take photos of you. Trust me. You don't want to get home and have hundreds of photos of the cool things you got up to, without you in them.

Friends

People often say that travelling as a couple can either make or break a romantic relationship, but few mention how travel can make or break a friendship.

Friendships can be equally amounts fulfilling and joyous, heartbreaking and maddening; but above all they can be fickle things. Take, for example, my best friend in high school. We've known each other since we were eight years old and I can't count the number of times I slept over at her house after maths study sessions, or the number of phone calls we made to each other to gossip about boys or talk about our dreams for the future. I thought we'd be friends forever, and we're still in touch on social media, but once high school ended and we discovered we were vastly different people, we naturally drifted apart. On the flip side, one of my closest friends right now is a woman I met when we were lumped together for a group assignment in university. We weren't particularly close then and now live in different states, but in the decade following university we've stayed in touch by having monthly phone conversations that last for hours. It's funny how friendships pan out, which makes travelling with friends incredibly high stakes: by trip's end, you're either sworn enemies fighting to send the other person home in a casket, or you've bonded so tightly you've become each other's chosen family. Tragically, there is no in between.

Friend,
I hardly knew ye

In my early twenties, I made the grave mistake of travelling with a new friend. Ours was the type of friendship that accelerated quickly: within months of knowing each other we were over at each other's homes for family dinners and spending weekends shopping and having movie nights.

When we saw sale flights for Japan advertised, we impulsively bought tickets. It was the perfect time for a holiday – I'd just broken up with my boyfriend and needed a distraction, and she was overworked and needed a break. I figured if anything went heinously wrong, we were only gone for a couple of weeks; how bad could things get?

The first part of the trip went wonderfully: we stuffed ourselves with cheap sushi, had fun getting lost in Tokyo's laneways, and relaxed in onsens together. But things quickly took a turn; I was still resentful towards my ex-boyfriend and she didn't know me well enough to know how to handle my moodiness, and I was irritated at having to constantly explain cultural norms to her because I was the Asian person in the duo (she was white).

Neither of us were at fault, but we weren't good enough friends to know how to communicate our discomfort to each other. And so we spent the remainder of our trip being overly polite, as if we weren't friends but strangers who just happened to share a room at our hostel.

When we said our goodbyes at the airport, we promised to see each other once we landed at home. 'I have to give you your twenty-first birthday present!' I told her. 'You have to come to my party!' she said. 'Message me once you get home.' When I texted her, she told me she was busy with a new job and would contact me again soon about her birthday party. Weeks became months, months became years, and years became a decade. I still have the present I bought for her.

Neither of us were at fault, but we weren't good enough friends to know how to communicate our discomfort to each other

ASIAN GIRLS ARE GOING PLACES

Sister from another mister

I've never quite understood the concept of having a 'best friend'; I come from a large family and am close with my siblings, so I've never wanted for that kind of company. So you can imagine my shock when I, quite unexpectedly, acquired a best friend in my twenties.

I met Corrie almost ten years ago, when we were introduced to each other as potential collaborators. We were instantly suspicious of each other as creatives who were part of the Chinese diaspora: were people only pairing us together because they didn't know any other Asian people? How dare people reduce us and our work to nothing but our cultural identities! Turns out, however, that those people were right! We immediately hit it off, and after hundreds of Sichuan hot pots, thousands of bottles of sake, and dozens of work trips where we were subjected to the acoustics of each other's violent bowel movements after eating the aforementioned Sichuan hot pots, we're practically blood sisters now. Aside from my family, she knows me better than anyone else and is the type of friend who will not shy away from telling me the truth, no matter how painful. (I once asked her what kind of fruit I resembled and she delivered an appraisal that was at once so swift and accurate it knocked the wind out of me: 'A lychee. You have defences that are easy to permeate and then people are met with a softness and sweetness that conceals a hardened, black heart.')

So when it came to the prospect of spending two months together in Los Angeles for work, I knew we would survive. Sure, there were struggles along the way, including ...

- the fact Corrie has a resting body temperature of 4000 degrees Celsius and must have bone-chilling air conditioning blasting at all times lest she stomp around the house howling bloody murder

- the evenings we were trapped inside our cockroach-infested Airbnb working on our laptops until midnight

- waiting for two hours to meet Mickey Mouse at Disneyland only to have the actor in the suit lose their patience with us (we very innocently wanted to pose behind Mickey with jazz hands, which the actor found inexplicably offensive, leading to some incredibly lackluster photos of us on the verge of tears after being admonished by a giant cartoon mouse)

- Corrie complaining that I am 'too loud' to live with (I like to sing made-up songs as I do housework, and she is an only child accustomed to deathly silence in her own home).

But even those moments have become fond memories, alongside recollections of slurping cold potato noodles and drinking nourishing, herbal bone broth in Koreatown; feeling badass hitting baseballs in a batting cage; marvelling at the walls of sugary American treats at Ralph's; exploring pumpkin patches during Halloween; scream-laughing at the kitchen knife we discovered in the drawer of my bedside table, which another guest had clearly left behind in the event of a home invasion; and spending hours sitting beside each other in comfortable silence as we scrolled on our phones. That is the sign of true friendship – being in each other's company without needing to engage with each other at all. We call ignoring each other while on our phones 'quiet time', despite the fact we're likely using that time to send each other stupid memes. It doesn't matter how far or close we are to each other in proximity; we chat to each other every day, even if it's just to say 'Hey'. In fact – I think that's her texting me right now.

Activities
with friends

1

Theme parks or local fairs. Suss out the carnival rides and food. If you're going to a theme park, do your research beforehand and create a loose itinerary based on which rides attract the longest lines; the novelty of going 'off the cuff' quickly wears off when people are tired, hungry and busting to use the toilet while waiting in hour-long queues.

2

Music festivals. They're the ultimate bonding exercise when you are drunk, tired, covered in mud, and euphoric from being in a crowd of music lovers. Have set meeting points for when you get separated from each other (phone reception can be terrible when thousands of people are trying to contact each other at the same time) and mind each other's food and drinks.

3

Get a manicure, pedicure or massage together.

4

Bar hopping or pub crawling.

5

Hikes or bouldering sessions. Help each other with your fitness goals and build trust doing activities that require active encouragement and backing.

6

Arcades! You'll have a brilliant time competing against each other in old-school arcade games.

7

Beach trips. Pack a picnic, plenty of sunscreen, and laze around like a herd of manatees.

8

Karaoke. The bigger the group the better, although I have been known to book a karaoke room with only one other friend. We weren't even intoxicated; we just had a lot of feelings that can only be expressed through the power of song.

9

Go to a sports match together.

10

Flea market trawling. Bring a backpack and stock up on interesting shopping finds unique to the area.

11

Take time out from each other.

12

Get psychic readings or, if you're feeling super adventurous, matching tattoos.

13

Check out a cat/ hedgehog/ bunny cafe. Take lots of photos!

14

Heading on a road trip? Make playlists that you can sing along to.

Life is not what you alone make it. Life is the input of everyone who touched your life and every experience that entered it. We are all part of one another.

Yuri Kochiyama,
American civil rights activist

Love and sex

Love and travel go hand in hand. When I think of romantic gestures I think of last-minute airport chases, sitting on someone's bike handlebars as soft rain drizzles, and letters penned between long-distance lovers. (Yes, I've been brainwashed by romantic movies, but can't a girl dream!) Some of the most romantic experiences I've had have been while travelling, and I still remember each of them fondly, despite the fact those relationships or flings ended.

On the flip side, being an Asian woman can inform your love life in less desirable ways too ... among the fond memories I have, I can also remember being catcalled and hit on by sleazy men as a single Asian woman travelling alone. I can also remember being caught in politically fraught situations with a white boyfriend because airport security guards refused to believe that we were a couple. Love, dating, sex and everything in between can be complex at the best of times and when you throw travel into the mix, there's never a dull moment.

Famous love and sex festivals around the world

DRAGOBETE, ROMANIA
The traditional Romanian love festival, celebrated on 24 February.

KANAMARA MATSURI, JAPAN
Find all things phallic at Tokyo's penis festival!

CARNIVAL, BRAZIL
Rio de Janeiro's infamous party – the biggest and wildest carnival in the world.

SYDNEY'S GAY AND LESBIAN MARDI GRAS, AUSTRALIA
Australia's renowned LGBTQIA+ parade and festival.

QIXI, CHINA
'Chinese Valentine's Day'. A love festival inspired by romantic mythology and celebrated since the Han dynasty.

FOLSOM STREET FAIR, USA
San Francisco's BDSM and leather subculture street fair.

The best apps for dating, love, and everything in between

While some travellers favour more traditional modes of seeking romance while on the go (bars, parties, or shimmying with someone on a dance floor), apps have made relationships (whatever kind you're after!) more convenient than ever. And if you're both adults and up-front and honest about what you're looking for, and you're being safe – go forth and make the most of modern technology!

Tinder (global)

One of the original dating apps. Swipe left to pass on someone, swipe right to match.

Weibo (China)

Post about yourself and what you're looking for and find like-minded singles with whom to connect.

Facebook Dating (global)

This is a dating profile separate to your regular Facebook user profile. Think Facebook Marketplace for singles.

Her (global)

While most dating apps have a sexuality preference (e.g., women seeking men, women seeking women), HER is a swiping app made specifically for queer women. Cisgender men are not allowed on HER.

Bumble (global)

Similar to Tinder and, in fact, founded by a co-founder of Tinder. This app is more female friendly, requiring women to make the first move to minimise any unsolicited, ahem, eggplant emojis and the like once they match with someone.

Hinge (global)

For users seeking more meaningful connections. Send people likes and learn more about each other through written prompts as well as photographs.

Badoo (South America, Europe and Africa)

A swiping and location-based app similar to Tinder that is big in European nations.

Climb every mountain

Climbing Mount Batur, an active volcano in Bali, was never on my bucket list. When I travelled to Indonesia with my boyfriend at the time, we had put together a dream list of activities and this – climbing a volcano that could spew molten lava at any time – was his. I was reluctant to begin with, but I felt good about our chances after learning it had been nearly two decades since Mount Batur's last eruption.

So the next morning, at 2am, we piled into a mini bus with other groggy climbers. (We'd be climbing in the darkness in order to reach the summit at sunrise.) As we sped along winding roads, we made friends with some of the other passengers, including a friendly French couple who had been travelling for some months, and you could tell – they had hardy, proper hiking gear and thermal clothing. It suddenly occurred to me that my boyfriend and I were woefully underprepared for the climb; we assumed that the mountain peak would be a similar temperature to its base – hot and humid – and so we were wearing nothing but shirts, shorts, and hoodies.

'We'll be fine,' my boyfriend assured me. I nodded and rested my head on his shoulder, sleeping for the remainder of the car ride. The climb was more gruelling than I expected, but each time I faltered, I felt my boyfriend behind me, physically pushing me upwards. At one point, he took my backpack, wearing two bags himself, so that I could forge ahead unencumbered.

Once we arrived at the top, woefully unprepared for the cold in the freezing, biting wind, he stripped off his jacket and bundled me up as he shivered in his thin shirt. The French couple were kind enough to lend him a jacket, but even then, we were still freezing. We huddled close together, sipping hot tea bought from our guides, as the clouds shifted to reveal the sun rising magnificently on the horizon. The tall grass around us swayed with the breeze as we held each other tight.

The world's most romantic destinations

Greece

Ah, the birthplace of Eros, the god of love! Take a stroll along Balos beach or enjoy a boat ride through the crystal-clear waters of the Blue Cave in Kastellorizo. Soak up the ancient history of the Acropolis or toast yourselves during a wine tour at the Olympia Land winery.

France

Visit the wall of love in Montmartre or marvel at the stained glass of the Sainte-Chapelle. Looking for something slower in pace? Laze and explore the old-school charm of Vieux Nice or head to the Bois de Boulogne and glide around Lac Inférieur in a private rowboat. And don't forget to sneak a kiss atop the Eiffel Tower before you go.

Iceland

Is there anywhere more magical than picturesque Iceland? Marvel at the northern lights, go horseback riding on black sand beaches in Vik, take a dip in Reykjavik's natural swimming pools, or do the short hike to the Reykjadalur Hot Springs.

Czech Republic

Embrace all things dramatic in Prague and take a stroll through the Vysehrad cemetery (the poet's cemetery) or book tickets to the opera (at the time of writing, Prague State Opera house has just been renovated). Then, instead of cruising across Vltava River at sunset, enjoy the view by walking from Prague castle across the Charles Bridge.

Namibia

For those lovers seeking natural wonders. Go hot air ballooning over the dunes in Sossusvlei, or enjoy a safari tour in Bwabwata National Park. In the early evening, observe the wild animals at Etosha watering hole, or the flamingos gathered at Walvis Bay. Break things up by going sandboarding in Swakopmund.

Switzerland

Get cosy with your loved one on the renowned Glacier Express or sip hot chocolate after carving up the snow on the Matterhorn. Then take a romantic walk along Montreux Lakeside before taking a tour at a famous Swiss chocolatier. My pick is Maison Cailler.

Morocco

Disconnect from the rest of the world by going camping or camel trekking in the Sahara Desert, or relax in the gardens at Jardin Majorelle. For something faster in pace, explore bustling Marrakesh and be part of the buzz at Jemaa el-Fnaa market.

Interview with Mithila Gupta

Mithila Gupta is an India-born, Aussie-grown screenwriter. She's recently written popular TV series such as *Bump, Five Bedrooms, The Unlisted* and many more. She loves a love story and dreams of taking over the world with her own slate of ambitious, uplifting and inclusive projects.

ML   What is your cultural background and how does it influence your approach to love and romance?

MG   I'm Indian – I was born in Jaipur, Rajasthan – a.k.a. 'The Pink City'... It's full of palaces, super romantic, still feels like old India. We moved to Melbourne, Australia, when I was four and I've grown up on Bollywood cinema as the most direct (and fun) access to my culture. Thanks to Bollywood I still speak fluent Hindi. Also thanks to Bollywood, I believe in perfect love – huge love – the kind of love that has you singing and dancing on cliff tops. I throw myself into love without too much thought but definitely too much optimism. It's beautiful. It can also be terribly disappointing when faced with the reality of the modern dating scene!

ML   Have you had any racist experiences on the dating scene and if so, how did you handle them? What was the outcome?

MG   Sure bloody have. I experienced outward racism as a romantic little girl, from the age of seven(ish) to sixteen – I was bullied, stood up, told I was a gorilla and teased for having a moustache. I was too young to accept it as racism ... mostly because I was so desperate to assimilate. And so, I simply believed I was gross. Once I got to university things changed. People saw themselves as more woke and all of a sudden I was hot property. Translation: I was exoticised by some. And yes, some just liked me 'cos I'm me, which is nice. I excused/ignored the exoticising in the beginning but as I got older I got wiser and stronger. It's a deal breaker for me now ...

So if you're trying to date me try not to tell me you love my chocolate skin or ask me about the *Kama Sutra*. Cheers.

ML   **When you're dating a non-Asian person, are you ever met with any judgement (from others, or even yourself) and if so, why do you think that is?**

MG   I didn't use to judge myself, but I am curious about my mostly white dating history. I don't think it's as simple as saying I've been brainwashed or colonised – because I have felt deep love (sometimes lust) for the Goras I have dated. It's something I'd like to dig into and research, even if it's just with my therapist. Luckily my parents have never judged me. The extended family and community may have, but I'm pretty immune to that because my parents have provided me with ... well, everything ... and theirs is the only opinion that matters to me. Mum loved my first partner (a Gora) so much. She used to feed him seven rotis in one sitting (Dad and I would have two each). My current partner is of Croatian heritage. His ethnicity has only come up as a positive aspect of him (generalised statements from Dad like 'Oh good, they are good family people' and 'Oh good, they eat good food'.)

So if you're trying to date me try not to tell me you love my chocolate skin or ask me about the *Kama Sutra*. Cheers.

ML   How do you navigate cultural differences with the person you're dating?

MG   Now I've found my voice (my backbone) I'm all about open communication. I am hugely proud of my heritage. It informs my career and also how I relate to people. On a date I'll naturally go on and on about India and if the dude is racist he won't come back for more. Yay. If I feel anxious or triggered or misunderstood on a date, I won't go back. Double yay. If I find mutual love and respect with someone I'll continue to speak up if needed, like if I feel 'other'ed or when India's killing it on the cricket pitch. And I expect the same from my partner if I 'other' them – minus the cricket bit.

ML   How do you manage hookups and casual flings when your Asian parents are traditional or conservative?

MG   We just don't talk about it. It's hilarious … My mum and dad will get on my dating apps with me. Dad can read a person's character on first glance so he's a great gatekeeper! But we have never spoken about sex. If it's a hookup, I tell them about the date and the story ends there. Or I say nothing. I was once brave enough to start a dating blog – but I called myself 'Miss M' and used a hell of a lot of innuendo for fear they'd dig it up. (Mum's favourite pastime is googling me, by the way.) In my early twenties I went to South America for four months with my partner. I told my parents we got separate beds. Of course they knew we didn't! But it's never spoken of. When I went on the pill I told them it was for period pain. Mum, Dad, if you are reading this – it was definitely for period pain.

ML   What is the best and worst experience you've had while travelling in a relationship?

MG   The best was the four months in South America with my ex. It was like travelling with my best friend. We partied, explored ... even got gastro at the same time. And we always took care of each other. I remember in Cuba we decided to take private salsa dancing classes together. After the first class it was clear he sucked and was hugely holding me back. So the next day he suggested I go alone and dance it out with the teacher. And it was the best, most intense and freeing dance I've ever had. I have my ex to thank for that.

The worst was a couple of years ago when a 'friend' convinced me to date him. We got excited and booked a trip to Fiji. Then the day before leaving, he dumped me and said he only wanted to go as friends. Dick move – but it was actually quite good because I still went (don't judge, I'm an Indian immigrant in Australia – I respect the value of money and also I'd been working seven days a week and needed the break) BUT I didn't give a fuck about his needs and did my own thing the entire time. Needless to say, we are no longer 'friends'.

ML   How do you survive a trip with a significant other without killing each other?

MG   Open communication is pretty much my solution to any problem. If something pisses you off, talk about it in that moment. Don't let it build up and then explode. And don't gaslight yourself and say it's not important. It's all important.

ML   What is the most romantic destination you've ever visited? What made it romantic?

MG   Jaipur. Because of the history. Because I know that's where life started for me.

ML   What is your ideal date, and where in the world would it be?

MG   I dream of taking someone I love to India with me. The ideal date would be our seven-day wedding with all of our family and friends and of course an elephant for the lucky man to arrive on. I'm a simple girl with simple needs.

ML   Do you have top tips or general advice when it comes to the intersection of love and travel?

MG   My general approach to dating, whether at home or beyond, is to be cautiously optimistic. And follow your gut. It's meant to be fun. If it doesn't feel fun, talk about it. If you can't talk about it, get rid of them and go back on your own or with friends who understand you.

Date ideas when you're on the go

1

Go to a farmer's market and cook each other a meal using local produce.

2

Get a cocktail on a rooftop and stargaze.

3

Be silly and indulge your inner kids by visiting a 'smash room' where you can throw plates, hit a computer with a baseball bat, and take a sledgehammer to a car bonnet (and more!) while wearing protective gear.

4

Go on a ghost tour and cling to each other for dear life.

5

Visit a legitimate (no 'Tiger King'–style businesses!) animal conservation reserve and sponsor an animal together.

6

Book unconventional accommodation. If you have the budget, go big! Check out bubble tents, Arctic igloo resorts, tree houses, and underwater hotels.

SELF-CARE

When it comes to your own wellbeing, the pre-flight safety demonstrations are correct: in an emergency situation (or, I would argue, in any situation) you should always prioritise your own health and safety before attending to others.

It's a radical concept for many women, let alone Asian women, who are so accustomed to self-sacrifice and ensuring everyone else's needs are met above all else. So strap yourself in and get ready for the adventure of a lifetime: it's called 'Putting yourself first'. It's an intimidating thought, but take some deep breaths. Grab my metaphorical hand. We're going to get through this together.

Health

Contrary to the stereotype of stoic, silent fathers who are in denial about their own health, my father is on top of his own physical health to the point that he goes for biannual check-ups and implores me and my siblings to see a doctor at the merest whisper of discomfort.

'I've had a bit of a headache today.'
Dad's advice? 'Go to the doctor.'

'Mosquitos bit me on the weekend!'
Dad: 'Have you booked a doctor's appointment?'

'I'm feeling fitter than I've ever felt in my life!'
Dad: 'For now – best to see a doctor.'

I get the sense that he's making up for lost time after being relatively unhealthy for much of his adult life: spending forty years running our family restaurants, eating badly, and sleeping irregularly. Sometimes he'd be so tired that he'd fall asleep upright as we were speaking to him. Since he's semi-retired

(do Asian fathers ever truly retire?), he's drilled it into us that if we don't have our health, we have nothing, especially when we're travelling. When you're on the go, you're thrown out of your regular routine, disrupting your dietary, sleep, and exercise habits. Medicines can also be missed or administered at incorrect times due to time differences, and changing climates can be a shock to the system. Emotionally, you're on high alert, being in situations where you are constantly problem solving and inundated with new stimuli. And now with the coronavirus, travelling and staying healthy can feel like an impossible feat, with each country having different regulations around quarantine and self-isolation, face masks, social distancing, and vaccination roll out schemes. So how do you stay healthy when the odds are seemingly stacked against you?

I take care of my physical health by acknowledging when I'm reaching exhaustion point and resting ... and also knowing where to get drinkable water. I care for my mental health by keeping diaries and going on solo walks.

Meg, South Korea

Jitterbug

Much like having children, travelling will not fix a struggling relationship – your problems will follow you wherever you travel unless you tackle them head-on with some self-reflection, accountability, and kindness.

That includes your relationship with yourself. I have chronic anxiety, something I developed when I was eleven years old, and there used to be nothing that sent me into a panic attack faster than an upcoming trip. Just knowing that I'd be meeting new people and entering unknown, unpredictable environments made me break out into a cold sweat; there have been instances of extreme anxiety I've had where I've been physically incapacitated, shaking from low blood sugar (when I'm anxious I feel nauseated and can't eat) and in tears on the floor. That said, not even disembarking a flight on a wheelchair due to almost fainting from anxiety will stop me from travelling! (Yes, this actually happened! Yes, it was a wakeup call! No, I have no regrets!)

Much of my own anxiety comes from wanting to please others, to ensure that the wants and needs of others are addressed before – and sometimes to the detriment of – my own. It's a very female thing; we're taught to nurture, and to hold ourselves up to incredibly high and often impossible standards for the sake and comfort of others. And despite mental illness still being a rather taboo subject, especially among Asian cultures, anxiety and depression feel more pervasive than ever – particularly in recent years where much of the world's population has been forced or encouraged to stay indoors and isolated from each other to prevent the spread of COVID-19. As I've gotten older, I've learned how to manage my anxiety around travel much better using the following methods. (Side note: my strategies are personal to my own mind and body, and are curated to my own needs after twenty years of individualised therapy, so they may not work for you. And any long-term measures should be discussed with your doctor or a mental health professional!)

It's a very female thing; we're taught to nurture, and to hold ourselves up to incredibly high and often impossible standards for the sake and comfort of others

Self-care
on the go

1

Have a set of breathing exercises that you can return to each time you feel yourself becoming overwhelmed. There are many apps available that offer guided breathing exercises. Breathe in through your nose and out through your mouth. (The reason why you can feel dizzy when you're anxious is that hyperventilation decreases the amount of carbon dioxide in your bloodstream. Breathing in through your nose helps regulate your breathing.)

2

Chill out with meditation, music, audiobooks, podcasts, or your favourite TV show.

3

Remind yourself that you are safe and then hold the image of your safe place in your mind's eye – this might be your bedroom, or a hammock on your balcony, or a certain beach.

4

Exercise! Exercise boosts serotonin and helps stabilise your mood. It also helps to work out anxious energy. Find a local gym or go for a jog in a park. If you're not feeling up for exercise, try stretching. Get back into your body and ground yourself in the present moment.

5

Be kind to yourself. When you're about to board that train, boat, or plane, indulge in your favourite snacks, buy some trashy gossip magazines, or a comfy neck pillow or face mask.

6

Pack your favourite soft toy or childhood object. It may sound juvenile, but it can make a huge difference to have a comfort item with you when you're travelling, especially if you're missing a significant other or pets at home.

I go to parks. Yangon (biggest city in Myanmar) can get you down but Maha Bandula Park (famous park in the middle of the city) really helps a gal relax.

Tammy, Australia

Slowing down

Modern living is, by virtue of the economic systems of which we're part, fast paced and unrelenting. I don't think I'm alone in saying that I rarely have time to reflect, or even take days off without feeling some level of guilt.

(When my psychologist said to me during one of our sessions, 'Michelle, relaxing is also a crucial part of working', I simply stared back at her blankly, astral projecting into the ether.) As an Asian person, I feel like I've had a strong work ethic drilled into me by my parents, who prided themselves on hard work above all else. And as an Asian woman, I feel a constant and perhaps unconscious need to prove myself – that I'm just as good as if not better than the men or non-Asian people beside me. It's an unhealthy mindset, but one that I've been conditioned to subscribe to: time is money, and money comes from productivity, so simply being, recuperating, or even being ill are indulgences.

As a result, whenever I fly long haul, I have a list of tricks in my arsenal to ward off the intense jetlag that will inevitably follow. These tricks include: setting my watch to the time at my destination and sleeping when it's 'bedtime' there; stretching regularly and going for strolls down the plane aisles; wearing compression socks and shoes that are easy to slip on and off so I don't become fatigued constantly tying and retying my shoelaces (it makes me cringe seeing other passengers plodding around barefoot – what are they picking up on those sticky carpets and bathroom floors?); eating and drinking water regularly; taking vitamin C, olive leaf extract, ArmaForce, or any other preventative supplements that will boost my immune system; and bringing comforting and light snacks to eat once I arrive at my destination to keep my blood sugar levels up. (My go-to snacks are instant miso soup or packet noodles, as you can depend on most kinds of accommodation having at least a kettle.)

When I'm travelling alone, this list is my saving grace, because the only person you have to depend on for your physical wellbeing is yourself. However, it wasn't enough to stave off the tickling feeling in my throat when I arrived in Dublin on an overcast, drizzly day in 2019. In the lead-up to the flight I'd been battling a number of overlapping deadlines and keeping my body in a prolonged and unsustainable state of 'I'm-about-to-fall-terribly-ill-if-I-pause-for-even-one-moment-so-I'll-just-keep-working-and-taking-vitamins-and-gargling-and-I'll-eventually-get-through-this!' in order to stay afloat, so I should have known that my body was on the precipice of burning out. As my taxi sped to my Airbnb in the city, I felt flushed with fever, a pressure headache pulsing at my temples. (Something

The only person you have to depend on for your physical wellbeing is yourself

I would check myself into hospital for IMMEDIATELY nowadays! Ah, simpler times.) I wanted nothing more than to sleep. But once I was dropped off, I had no choice but to drag myself out and stock up on medication, tissues, herbal teas, and pre-made soups. I was determined to nip this illness in the bud: I'd travelled this far, had never been to Ireland, and I had a strict itinerary to adhere to. I was in the country for work and had purposely arrived a week early in order to sightsee and explore, knowing that I'd be occupied for the rest of my trip. I had an inbox bursting with recommendations from friends that I was dying to use, and had lofty plans for my free time: taking a bus to the Cliffs of Moher, ducking over to Cork, kissing the Blarney Stone, and getting drunk and eating a traditional stew with soda bread at the Guinness Storehouse. But within hours, I was overcome: sneezy, congested, bleary eyed, and lethargic. I gave in, changed into my pyjamas, and slept for twelve hours. I was sick for a week, and while I was sorry for myself the first several days – scared and isolated on my own, and feeling lonely and craving my creature comforts, like a shower I actually knew how to operate (what is it about showers in foreign countries that makes you feel as angry and befuddled as the bone-wielding apes in *Space Odyssey*?) – I eventually accepted that I needed to lean in to my recovery, to lower my expectations of myself, and let my body heal. So I slept, tuned into local television stations and marvelled at their programming, and read books that I'd meant to read on the plane but never got around to because there were a million movies to watch and other passengers to defeat at Tetris. I ate when I felt like it and kept my fluids up. Without anything else to focus on but myself and my own wellbeing, I genuinely began to enjoy my period of recuperation; it felt good to slow down and let my mind ease into the pace of my body, which had for so long been crying out to be cared for.

Anywhere in nature listening to natural sounds is my thing. If it is by a water body, then it is even better. While it is always lovely to have company, it is such spaces where I reconnect with myself. I am absolutely fascinated by wildlife, especially the ones that are smaller. I love bugs and ferns and all the little things that surprise me. Just looking at them and imagining how quickly their lives are moving compared to mine. It is a sense of wonder that relaxes me the most.

Anonymous, Ireland

Interview with Asami Koike

Asami Koike is the founder of Shapes and Sounds, an online platform that talks about Asian Australian mental health and wellbeing. With work experience in trauma-informed mental health care and yoga, Asami leads conversations about mental health that interweave topics like race, gender and culture.

ML What is your cultural background and how does it shape your approach to your own health?

AK I am a first-generation Japanese immigrant living in Australia. For a long time, I never really thought about my health in relation to my background, but over the last few years, I've started to appreciate the ties that I have to my ancestry. Japanese people are known to have really long life expectancies so I'm trying to learn more about the food, spirituality and aesthetics of Japanese culture to learn the secrets to good health!

ML What drives your interest in wellbeing?

AK When I was eighteen, I entered into a six-year relationship with an eating disorder. It was during this time that I realised that you can 'fix' your physical symptoms (in my case, stabilise my weight) but that doesn't necessarily equate to feeling 'well'. In other words, we can be absent of physical symptoms but there's another level of work that we need to do to experience vitality and wellbeing. It's this visceral memory that drives my interest in wellbeing – what is that 'other bit' that we need to nurture so that we can feel truly alive?

ML Shapes and Sounds is a mental health resource for Asian diasporas living in Australia. Why is appealing to that demographic (Asians living in a Western country) important to you?

AK It took me only five years of working in the mental health and community sectors to notice that there's a lack of culturally responsive mental health care in our current system. When you see, firsthand, young Asian Australians falling through the cracks in our service delivery or being treated unfairly by unknowingly racist and ignorant workers and services, something shifts in you and you think, how is this in any way acceptable in our so-called 'multi-cultural' society?

Witnessing this shook me to the core so I started writing about Asian Australian mental health and it struck a chord with many in the Asian Australian community. It made me realise that we were craving these intersectional conversations about mental health: conversations that acknowledge factors like our cultural backgrounds, our family dynamics and the expectations and assumptions placed upon us (both internally and externally) as Asian people in Australia.

ML   Why is having Asian women at the centre of your practice significant?

AK   When I look around at the mental health, wellbeing and social justice spaces, I see mostly women. I think we are naturally more reflective and we have the ability to articulate our experiences into language. I think Asian women often hold this space in families, where the men are quiet and the women do all the chatting on behalf of the men. Don't get me wrong, I think that dynamic sucks, but I think that if we have the resources to create conversation around topics like Asian mental health, then we definitely should use that strength to help not only ourselves but people of all genders in our community.

ML   Are there specific mental health challenges that come with being an Asian woman?

AK   Funny you ask this because there is research that points out that Asian women (born and raised in America) were the group at highest risk of suicide in the US. This definitely indicates specific mental health challenges that come with being an Asian woman, and it's interesting to see that this is actually exacerbated by the diaspora experience.

I think many Asian women raised in the West still face the assumptions and expectations of their (or their parents') ancestral country about what it means to be a 'good woman'. Add in the experiences of being fetishised by the white gaze and then dismissed or overlooked at work one too many times, and you may have a little recipe for disaster.

What becomes even more dangerous is when someone in this situation seeks mental health

I focus on caring for my health by finding ways to stay grounded and centred so that I can really 'be' where I am support from someone who doesn't have a culturally responsive practice. Common Eurocentric advice, like 'create strong boundaries with your family', and 'find ways to build up your confidence at work', can be really dismissive because there's no acknowledgement of the cultural norms of many Asian cultures. I'm sure many people can understand that setting boundaries with our Asian parents doesn't quite work like it does for our Caucasian peers, or that we understand that we don't speak up at meetings as a sign of respect to those senior to us. When we seek mental health support only to find that 'it didn't work', we can feel even more isolated and alone, which then leaves us in a really dangerous situation.

ML   **Why is it important for Asian women to put their own health first and foremost?**

AK   When Asian women prioritise themselves, they're actively resisting oppression and changing the world. I'd go as far to say that every single time an Asian woman chooses herself before her partner, before her family, before her work, she's dismantling the status quo.

Sometimes I think that the world is stacked against us as Asian women. You're a woman so you may face the same glass ceiling barriers as all other women, but you're also often culturally expected to be of service to your family, your husband and your children.

I've definitely seen the impact of women who abandon themselves for the sake of others' comfort and I've also seen what it looks like when women choose to prioritise themselves. There's a level of risk involved when prioritising yourself and oftentimes you're ostracised or a little shunned by your family/community. But, in saying so, the impact of abandoning yourself and becoming unwell creates far greater problems for you and everyone around you in the long run.

ML   **Travelling can be exhausting, taking a toll on our bodies, minds and hearts. What is your advice for staying physically and mentally fit when you're on the move?**

AK   I usually have a really solid weekly routine that consists of yoga, self-reflection, walking, etc., so when I'm travelling, I actually just let all of that go (most importantly, without any guilt) so that I can be fully present to the adventures I'm facing.

I focus on caring for my health by finding ways to stay grounded and centred so that I can really 'be' where I am. And when I do this, I can tell when I need to take a nap, or skip an adventure, or eat more vegetables or stop drinking for a while.

ML   **You're a yoga teacher who has taught around the world. What are some of the best poses to do when you're in a confined space, like a hotel room, plane, or train carriage?**

AK   Supported viparita karani or otherwise known as 'legs up the wall' is a good one. I find that I walk a lot more when I'm travelling compared to my usual life so anything that helps to balance all of that downward movement really helps me to sleep easy and wake up somewhat refreshed the next day.

All you need to do is sit at ninety-ish degrees but with your legs on the wall and your back on the floor. Try to get your hips as close to the wall as you can, and you can even prop your hips up on a pillow to support your lower back.

If it feels great, take some deep breaths for a few minutes while you're slightly upside down, or play around with different leg placements. You might like to keep your knees bent, your hips further away from the wall, or you might want to do this lying on the bed or even without a wall at all … see what works for your body.

Now that I'm at an age where my body is decaying faster than it is growing, I do feel inclined to say, don't force this or try things that you're not really used to when you're on the road. If physical movement is in your regular life, see what you can keep up during your travels, otherwise, don't stress your body out more by doing any new stretches or activities that might contribute to any pre-existing niggles.

Instead, you could think about taking the time out to centre and ground yourself with some dedicated meditation or breath work time. Even just taking a few deep, full breaths with a soft, moving belly can help all the organs get a nice squeeze as well as keeping you grounded and calm as you process a ton of new information while you're travelling.

Don't force this or try things that you're not really used to when you're on the road

ML   Do you have any resources or activities that you recommend for maintaining your physical and mental health when you're travelling?

AK   I do usually travel with my little physio/tennis ball just in case something feels really off in my body. I also take lots of photos as a way to document what I'm doing and then I look through the day's photos at the end of the day as a way to process all that new information. I often also take a big social media break when I'm travelling (as in, I'll post stuff but I won't look through social media or reply to anyone) which really helps me to feel like I'm disconnected and I can really focus on myself for a while.

ML   What does self-care mean to you?

AK   Self-care for me is really all about becoming the carer for myself. That means planning my meals in advance, or cooking (PS I hate cooking), or keeping my finances in check, or making sure I get to work on time, or being my own coach/mentor/cheerleader etc.

Self-care for me is all about being intentional in my actions. I continually ask myself, am I responding or am I reacting here? Why do I feel a certain way? Does this work for me or do I need something different? I find that it's this continual cultivation of self-awareness that is ultimately my self-care.

Self-care is a commitment to myself that I will prioritise my own health and wellbeing so that I can be well in my relationships with all the people around me.

Safety

As an Asian woman, I'm normally underestimated unless I'm haggling over seafood at the markets or chiding someone for being unable to make a meal from memory (the measurements should be in your head; you don't need a recipe).

Generally speaking, I'm not afforded much respect. Because when people meet me, they expect that I'll be the stereotype of an Asian woman that they've constructed in their minds: demure, delicate, deferential, and deathly terrified of the sun. Sure I can be all of those things and often all at once, but none of those characteristics actually define me as a person! However, that doesn't stop people from trying to take advantage of me, particularly when I'm travelling and in an unfamiliar environment. I'm a rather hypervigilant traveller but I've still had con artists attempt to scam me in Spain, traffic police in Indonesia stop me for bribes, and had people brush up against me, grope me, or photograph me without my consent in public, in many countries. Beyond that, I'm often spoken to loudly and rudely (when people assume I can't speak English) or called outright racist slurs.

Now, the global outbreak of the coronavirus has led to East Asians being vilified more than ever. And thanks to certain world leaders who went to great lengths to refer to the coronavirus as the 'Chinese' virus, there was a huge spike in violent anti-Asian attacks around the world, particularly in the United States. These attacks are meant to intimidate, to make Asian people feel small and ashamed, but I refuse to be afraid.

Put it down to being born in the Year of the Horse, but I've always had a strong sense of social justice and a willingness to fight for it. Which has led me down some dangerous paths like ...

— the time I was at a nightclub and fly kicked a man who refused to leave my friend alone and was saved by security just as the man was coming to knock me out

— ... or the time I yelled at catcallers so loudly that pedestrians stopped to watch

— ... or when I chased a pickpocket in Barcelona demanding my money back

— ... or when I hunted down and screamed at a peeping tom who was filming me in a public toilet.

The point is – I wouldn't recommend my own methods, so I've sought the advice of some smarter and much more competent Asian women to share their methods instead. And while these tips do, unfortunately, apply as much at home as when you're travelling, they're particularly useful when you're in an unfamiliar place.

Interview with Eva Chin & Kim Lawton

Eva Chin is a second dan black belt who works in insurance finance. She lives in Australia with her partner, Kim, who is a first dan black belt and works as an insurance specialist. They are fur mums to a big thirteen-year-old ginger cat called Pedro. They enjoy travelling, eating and keeping (relatively) fit.

ML   What is your cultural background and how has it shaped your attitude towards personal safety?

EC   My cultural background is Malaysian Chinese. Personal safety wasn't a big focus growing up, because we lived on the Sunshine Coast – a quiet coastal town, one where you could leave your front door open all night and still feel safe. My dad was raised on a rubber plantation (so my mum tells me) and is a country boy at heart and easily trusts people. My mum is also a trusting person and quite optimistic about things, and in my opinion can sometimes be naïve when it comes to people's intentions. My parents' easy, trusting nature, combined with my quiet upbringing, has resulted in a relaxed attitude towards personal safety, which I still carry with me to this day.

KL   My background is Filipino Australian. Safety has always been a top priority for me growing up as I was raised by a single parent and helped raise my younger brother.

ML   You're both black belts. (Please don't hurt me.) What kind of martial arts did you study, and what inspired you to pursue that path?

EC   I started practising Taekwon-Do when I was ten years old. As a kid, I was always interested in martial arts, inspired by the many Bruce Lee, Jackie Chan and Hong Kong–produced martial arts movies that I watched growing up. It was my dad's decision to have my brother and I start Taekwon-Do. He felt that as Asians growing up in a Western society, learning martial arts would mean we would be able to defend ourselves should the need arise. I studied it for fifteen years.

KL I also studied Taekwon-Do, this is where Eva and I met actually. I've always had a love for martial arts – I was basically a tomboy growing up. Like Eva, I was pretty obsessed with martial arts films and loved Bruce Lee, he was one of my childhood idols. I started Taekwon-Do at nineteen to increase my fitness, but mainly to learn self-defence. I think it's important that all women know how to protect themselves.

ML **You're a gay couple. Have you ever encountered any homophobia on your travels that made you feel unsafe? How did you tackle it?**

EC No, I don't think we have ever experienced homophobia. We have had the awkward experience (on a few occasions) where we've booked a double bed only to have the receptionist tell us it's an error and try to give us two single beds.

I think we haven't experienced homophobia on our travels because, firstly, we don't look stereotypically gay, so you wouldn't be able to tell we were a gay couple right away. I think a lot of people would assume we are friends or sisters.

Secondly, we are discreet when in unfamiliar environments or when we travel as we are both small in build and do not want to attract unwanted attention.

Thirdly, I like to research our travel destinations and will avoid travelling to any cities/countries that are not gay friendly. As much as we would love to visit every country, there are some countries that are not safe for gay couples, and I'm happy to not visit those countries. (They also don't deserve my hard-earned dollars going into their economy.)

ML   **What should you do if someone is catcalling you?**

EC   I either ignore it or death stare them (I have a mean resting bitch face). These people are simpletons and don't deserve my time and attention. I'm a big believer in 'we can't control how others behave, but we do have control over how we respond'.

KL   I also try and ignore it if I can, but if I can't I would give them a look and tell them to f*ck off.

ML   **What should you do if someone is following you?**

EC   Thankfully I've never been in this situation before. If you're in a dark, quiet street, I would quicken my pace and look back every so often at the person following me. This lets them know that I'm aware they're following me. I would also be searching for my keys or something to use as a weapon and have my phone handy. Phones usually have an SOS safety function, so it's important to know how to activate yours.

We were taught in Taekwon-Do that a loud, aggressive shout is a form of self-defence. If someone is following you and they get close – turn around, shout as loudly, deeply and aggressively as you can (in Taekwon-Do we call it a 'kihap'), and run. Hopefully the shout stuns them and gives you a head start (if needed).

I've also read in an article that if you engage with the potential assailant (e.g., by looking them in the eye, or asking them a simple question like what the time is), they are less likely to attack you as they're aware that you're aware of them and may be able to identify them.

KL   I agree with Eva, shouting works! I've been followed before and the guy kept getting closer and closer. When the guy was within 1.5 metres, I turned around and shouted 'YAA', in a ready to fight stance. He was so startled he ended up walking away in shock. I think having your phone ready and texting a family member about what's happening is a good idea and always look back to identify the person and be aware of your surroundings.

ML   **When you're travelling in a new environment, what are the things you should be taking note of when it comes to your own personal safety?**

EC   Some things we do when travelling (I've also travelled alone overseas and interstate for work and leisure) is when checking into a hotel, protect your room number. Do not let anyone know your room number. The little card that hotels sometimes slip your room key into usually has your room written on it – put that away so no one can see it.

I sometimes try to make it appear as if I'm not travelling on my own by asking for a second room key. Be aware of hotel staff – they may be providing potential assailants with information.

Trust your gut. If it doesn't feel right, it probably isn't. Get yourself out of the situation. Always know where your exits are.

Be alert, be aware, and act confidently. Look around and look people in the eye. I think if you appear alert, aware and confident, you are less likely to become a target.

I tend to pay more attention to people than other aspects of my surroundings (it helps that I love to people watch). I am always watching people and scanning for unsavoury characters and situations.

And don't drink too much if out in an unfamiliar environment. It's best to have your wits about you.

ML   **What basic self-defence moves should every woman know, regardless of their fitness level and age?**

EC   It's good to have a basic understanding of the body. What bends and what doesn't bend. What snaps and where. Where the weapons and weak points on the body are. You don't need to do self-defence to know this – you can experiment (gently) on your own body.

For those untrained in self-defence – knees and elbows are good weapons. The elbow is the strongest part of the body and is especially good in close situations. Bend your arm and swing those elbows like a crazy lady.

A few things we were taught in Taekwon-Do:

— **Eyes:** Go for the eyes. Gouge, scratch, poke.

— **Nose:** If you hit someone on the nose, their hands will usually reflexively go to their face.

— **Bite**: Bite if you have to, but if you can, try to bite through clothes (so you don't pick up anything nasty).

— Use anything around you as a weapon – a handful of dirt off the ground can be thrown in an assailant's face.

— **The fingers:** especially the pinkie finger – it's weak and can be snapped back easily. If you can, grab a finger and wrench it in a direction it doesn't normally go in.

— Kicking the **groin** is usually taught, but this can be risky if you're not a confident kicker or miss the target.

— You need to be high energy in self-defence situations, so invoke the inner psycho and don't forget to shout.

KL   Definitely learn how to get out of an arm- or behind-the-back grab. If you are going to attack, always put one hundred per cent into it and if you're overpowered relax first, play dumb with your hands up, then strike hard when the time is right.

ML   **Do you have any top tips or general advice for staying safe while travelling?**

KL   We always let family know where and when we're travelling. We limit activities at night and anything off our planned itinerary. Also, if you have an iPhone, activate Find my Friends so your location can be found if anything is to happen.

For those untrained in self-defence – knees and elbows are good weapons

MEMORABLE

Finding gold
TAMMY, AUSTRALIA

An experience that restored my faith in humanity was travelling to refugee camps along the Thai–Burma (Myanmar) border. People who work in these camps are some of the most selfless people you will ever come across. There is also an immense appreciation for life in these camps, especially amongst refugee children and youth.

Theft! Burglary!
GRACE, JAPAN

Creepy, but having my undies stolen at a laundromat.

MOMENTS

Reconnecting

ILDIKO, CANADA

My mother [who is Hungarian] got to reunite with her family in Hungary after losing contact with them for around fifty years. It came at a good time for her as her mother had passed away years before, and her sister passed away only months before the reunion, so she had lost her last connection to her family, history, and culture. The tears, joy and Hungarian banter was so touching and gave my mother new life in some respects.

CULTURE

AND FOOD

When I reflect on the places I've travelled to, I have trouble remembering specific details about locations or the people I met there.

I don't remember how crowded it was at the Colosseum, what accents waitstaff spoke with in restaurants, or the dimensions of a cliff face or temple. Instead, I'm the type of person who remembers the culinary impressions and sensations of a place: eating fresh rambutans on the roadside in Malaysia and letting the juice run down my arms, or the briny smell of live seafood at the Tsukiji market in Japan, or eating jamón ibérico on a freshly baked white bread roll in Spain. To me, food and culture are inextricably linked – it's ritual, it's memory, it's the best part of being alive.

Culture

As I've gotten older, there are some aspects of being a Chinese woman that I strictly adhere to and others I've learnt to softly reject in order to assert my own independence.

The principles I do adhere to revolve around Confucian principles of filial piety. I believe my parents have given me everything and so I must spend my own life repaying that debt as well as paying respects to my elders who have passed. I always serve my parents and older relatives first. I do not call my siblings by their actual first names and find it cringeworthy when I must. And I have superstitions surrounding that dastardly number, four. Beyond that, I believe meals are for sharing, sitting bare-bottomed on a toilet seat that isn't in my own home is a sure-fire road to disease, and wearing shoes indoors is a crime punishable by death.

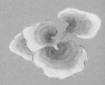

However in most other ways I live by codes that are relatively progressive, and I reject the patriarchal social systems in which I've been raised. So I don't believe I'm inferior to a man in any sense: I'd be proud to financially support my future family; I'd prefer my future children to carry my surname; I enjoy travelling alone despite the protests and concerns of more traditional relatives; and when waiters speak only to my brothers I simply speak louder until they listen because I am the one ordering for the table. (Oh – I also once asked my siblings for a clock as a birthday present. In Chinese culture, clocks as a gift are a no-no since 'giving a clock' sounds exactly like 'going to a funeral'. And then the clock smashed! But I am still alive to tell the tale. For now.)

However when I'm travelling, part of the joy of being immersed in another culture is setting aside some of my own personal attitudes and 'doing as the locals do' in order to be respectful and maximise my own experience. Whether that's dressing more modestly and covering my hair when I'm entering religious sites, kissing people on the cheek as a greeting (something I personally hate!), or eating whatever (and however much) food is put in front of me when I'm a guest in someone's house – I try my hardest to be accommodating. I say this after having seen too many travellers being arrogant or patronising towards other cultures and their customs (cough, white folks in Asian countries), which is not only disrespectful, but actually detracts from the traveller's experience and signals a lost learning moment. The best thing you can do to soak up another culture while travelling is to keep an open mind, be considerate of others, and of course – take house slippers with you wherever you go!

You must learn to be still in the midst of activity and vibrantly alive in repose

Indira Gandhi,
former prime minister of India

How to not be a jerk to other cultures

1

If you're in Russia, save your smiles for private moments with loved ones. Smiling in public in Russia can be perceived as inauthentic or shifty so keep those pearly whites hidden unless you want to intentionally freak someone out.

2

If you're catching a bus in New Zealand or Australia, it's customary to say 'thank you' and give a friendly wave to the driver when you alight. It's the equivalent of giving a courtesy wave when you're changing lanes on the road.

3

Avoid swearing in the US. As someone who is naturally foul-mouthed, I learnt the hard way (many awkward silences, and my American friends going bright red with horror) that even the most liberal Americans can find swear words downright offensive.

4

In Japan, eating while walking is a big no-no. Showing respect to your food is significant in Japanese culture, so if you're snacking in public, stop and smell the roses while you're wolfing down that onigiri.

5

In Germany and Sweden, there's no such thing as being 'fashionably late'. If you're not on time you're simply late and therefore unforgivably rude. This is the general rule in professional and social settings, so make sure you set a million alarms in the morning!

6

In Western countries cutting in line is generally considered quite rude, so if you want to avoid a tussle or, at the very least, some intensely withering stares, it's best to stay put and be patient.

7

Always use cutlery when dining in Brazil or Chile. If you're not using cutlery, at the very least wrap your food in a serviette rather than holding it with your bare hands. (What with the pandemic it's not a bad idea anyway – I love eating with my hands but since COVID-19 I'm wary of doing so, even after my hands have been sanitised ten times!)

8

Think twice before giving the thumbs up in the Middle East. It may be an inoffensive and even positive gesture in some cultures, but in many Middle Eastern countries it's basically the equivalent of giving the middle finger. Whoops.

Lunar New Year

When I think of Lunar New Year, I think of my Ma Ma. And I can see her as she was at the Lunar New Year celebrations during my childhood – standing at the stove at my father's house, checking on steaming pots, pressing buttons on beeping appliances, and seasoning pans that would spit and sizzle at her command.

As Ma Ma cooked, my siblings and I would lay a plastic tablecloth over the dining table and help set down each dish with reverence: steamed fish, sweet and savoury sesame balls (which my siblings and I would hold up to the light, our hands greasy, trying to find our favourite flavours), Buddha's delight, poached chicken and turnip cakes. For dessert, Ma Ma would bring out a tray of sliced oranges and watermelon. And once everyone was uncomfortably overfed, she would finally sit down with us and take a bite of fruit. She'd smack her lips together while eating watermelon and say with satisfaction, 'Very sweet'.

As I got older and Ma Ma became frailer, she stopped making these decadent Lunar New Year banquets. And so my siblings and I would celebrate by going out to restaurants with friends, or being adopted by other Chinese friends and their families. As adults, we'd ask Ma Ma, 'Remember when you used to make steamed orange sponge cake? Remember when you used to hand-make cheong fun?' and she'd shake her head, slightly dazed, and say, 'I never did that', before going back to watching television, or playing mah jong, or scrubbing her feet in a bucket of boiling water. My Ma Ma passed away one year ago; she was my last surviving grandparent. My favourite food in the world is her glutinous rice dumplings wrapped in sweet potato leaves, which my sisters and I filmed her making before she died. Next Lunar New Year, I'll make a plate of them for myself.

My favourite food in the world is her glutinous rice dumplings wrapped in sweet potato leaves

Where to celebrate Lunar New Year

A brief list of both Eastern and Western cities where LNY celebrations go big, to get you thinking!

Beijing

Spring Festival is the biggest day of the year in China, with millions of people migrating across the country to celebrate with family. Marvel at firework displays, lion dances, and traditional folk performances before tuning into the famous CCTV *New Year's Gala* – the most watched television program in the world.

Sydney

Head over to Darling Harbour in the morning to cheer on the rowers at the dragon boat races before a mouth-watering New Year's banquet in Chinatown. Fill the hours in between with Lunar New Year–themed art installations dotted across the city, live entertainment, and interactive workshops for all ages.

Singapore

Visit the iconic River Hongbao festival (normally held at Marina Bay) for food and photo opportunities, or check out the Chingay Parade where you'll be bowled over by a procession of music, dance and acrobatic performances from around the world joining to celebrate the city-state's multiculturalism.

San Francisco

With over one third of the population in San Francisco having Asian heritage, you better believe that the city's Lunar New Year celebrations are going to be next level. Highlights include the New Year parade, shopping at the flower market fair, and the Miss Chinatown Pageant (why not enter if you're eligible!).

Ramadan

You mightn't have considered travelling during the holy month before. After all, travelling in and of itself can be exhausting, let alone when you're fasting and potentially sleep deprived. But it may be getting out of your comfort zone that promotes a deeper self-reflection and connection to your faith, and/or leads to insights into other cultures and their customs. And just think of how every iftar could be different, depending on where in the world you may be: you could be feasting on endless bowls of kolak, or spoonfuls of creamy knafeh, some crispy jalebi fresh from the fryer, or platters of vibrant kuih ... can you tell I'm a sweet tooth? Here's a short list of cities to get you inspired if you're considering travelling during Ramadan:

- Kuala Lumpur, Malaysia

- Cape Town, South Africa

- Mashhad, Iran

- Abu Dhabi, United Arab Emirates

- Istanbul, Turkey

- Marrakesh, Morocco

- Cairo, Egypt

- Singapore

Note: If you're visiting a Muslim-majority country during Ramadan, like many of the above, make sure you do some solid research into store and restaurant opening hours beforehand, as these will have likely changed during the month. And pack some emergency snacks just in case you find yourself stranded for iftar!

Diwali

During the pandemic, the world has felt like a heavy and sombre place at times. India was rocked by COVID-19, putting a strain on cultural and spiritual festivals that normally act to unite communities. So, ironically, it feels like Diwali needs to be celebrated more than ever, if only to serve as a reminder that hope, joy and light will ultimately prevail over darkness and evil. As the world begins slowly opening up again, we'll be able to reunite in ways that honour the tragedy of the pandemic, as well as rejoice in the coming together of people again.

While Diwali is celebrated worldwide, India is the place to be if you want to get the full festival experience. Each city observes Diwali in diverse ways that are informed by religion and tradition. You could spend the five days of the festival in one of the following cities, or even split your time between a couple. Or (!) dispose of this list entirely and go on your own Diwali adventure.

To get you started, here's a small list of cities where Diwali celebrations sparkle. Head to:

- Jaipur to take in folk performances and wander beautifully decorated late-night markets

- Amritsar to see the glittering makeover given to the Golden Temple

- Varanasi, the spiritual capital of India, to witness thousands of oil lamps floating along the Ganges

- Udaipur to behold the breathtaking sight of glowing lanterns released into the sky

- Ayodhya, the birthplace of Lord Rama, to enjoy grand fireworks or laser shows.

'My favourite cultural festival'

Thingyan

TAMMY, AUSTRALIA

The water festival celebrating Burma (Myanmar)'s New Year. I have spent a lot of time travelling back and forth from Burma within the last ten years. The humidity in Burma is difficult to forget. On bad days it can feel like you're being suffocated and on good days it feels like your clothes have just come out of the washing machine. In some ways it feels irresponsible to be firing water out of cannons but on the other hand it reminds me of the really joyful moments in a place that has witnessed so much pain. The water symbolises the washing away of the previous year's bad luck.

Ganesh Chaturthi

ANONYMOUS, IRELAND

This is a festival where the elephant-headed god is worshipped. People come together and celebrate as a community. There are exorbitant pandals (tents) and idols of Ganesha all over the city or town. There are celebrations in the form of choreographed dances, dramas and folk story telling. However, the most fun is the freeform parade where the dhols (drums) beat to local popular tunes and people dance like there is no tomorrow as they carry the idols to the nearest water body to send off till next year. The opulence of festivities is worth witnessing; the sense of community and family is best seen in such festivals. Other such festivals are Durga Puja in Kolkata and Kumbh Mela. Also, one more thing! Kumbh Mela is the largest gathering of people that happens every twelve years! If you have not seen a mass festivity in India, you have missed something in life.

Gion Matsuri in Kyoto

ILDIKO, CANADA

The festival of Yasaka Shrine is very beautiful and special. Everyone walks the streets in their yukata (summer kimonos). The weather is sublime and there are parades with floats (Yamaboko Junko) in the streets! The festival dates back to 869 as a religious ceremony to appease the gods during the outbreak of an epidemic. A local boy is selected as a divine messenger and cannot set foot on the ground from the 13th July until he is paraded through the town on the 17th July. I bought a yukata and felt a great sense of pride and belonging there.

Food

As the child of restaurateurs, food is everything to me. Food is what brings families and communities together; it punctuates the day and makes milestones and ceremonies special; and, above all, it's delicious.

In my incredibly biased opinion, Asian people do food the best; our ingredients are fresh and bursting with flavour, and our cooking practices are as diverse as our cultures, so there is always a new dish to discover.

Several years ago, my family was joined by my white brother-in-law on a trip to visit extended family in Hong Kong. After a few hours of hanging out with us, he complained, 'Can we do something else? All your family does is eat, and then walk to another place to eat, before going somewhere else to eat some more.' At the time, we were walking to a restaurant after snacking on some curried fish balls from a street vendor. Technically, he wasn't wrong. But all the same, we turned to him, narrow-eyed (actually narrowed – not just our resting faces), and hissed, 'Yes? Is there a problem?' Asian people are food obsessed and travel has only contributed to the proliferation of that obsession. Due to centuries of sea trade, colonisation, and migration, Asian food can be found all over the world, from laksas in Australia's Northern Territory to pakoras in England to banh mis in Paris and rijsttafel in the Netherlands. Asians are the ultimate foodies and have insatiable appetites – by which I mean to say, there will be plenty of future trips for my brother-in-law to look forward to!

Your buffet battle plan

Is there any greater Asian tradition than the all-you-can-eat buffet? Whether it's a hotel breakfast buffet, a guided tour that ends with a feast of authentic local fare, or a dining hall full of bain-maries at your cousin's destination wedding, it always pays to have a plan that satisfies both your stomach and your wallet.

STEP 1   If you are dining with extended family members, and you have brothers who are also present, take a seat at the foot of the table. Your relatives will likely pass you over in conversation in favour of your inherently more fascinating brothers (unless they feel like interrogating you about your love life or pregnancy plans), but there is an upside to this. Being ignored gives you more time to focus on the mission at hand: EATING.

STEP 2   Begin with seafood. Construct a mountain of sea creatures and assign extra plates for discarded shells that can be handed to wait staff intermittently. Have one bowl filled with fresh water for handwashing.

STEP 3   Do not, under any circumstances, put any form of carbohydrate on your plate. Carbohydrates are cheap and you have rice at home.

STEP 4   Move on to land and sky meats.

STEP 5   If you must eat vegetables, eat only those vegetables that are difficult to prepare at home.

STEP 6   Break for fifteen to thirty minutes. Repeat steps 2 to 5 at least twice. If you fear judgement from staff or patrons, simply modify your outfit in subtle ways to convince less discerning folks that you are in fact, someone else – a scarf, a pair of sunglasses or fancy hat will do nicely.

STEP 7   Take your first sip of water. No more than half a cup! This is a palate cleanser only.

STEP 8   Choose one small serving of every single dessert.

STEP 9   Fill your pockets with candy and teabags.

STEP 10   Argue over the bill.

STEP 11   Go back to your accommodation and have explosive diarrhea.

'The best meal on my travels'

Cheap and local

TAMMY, AUSTRALIA

I love small, local eateries. Ones that particularly stand out include non-profit organisations that run cafes in places like Mae Sot, on the Thai–Burma (Myanmar) border, or within small villages in Burma. I think the cheapest meals are the best ones!

Cliche but true

GRACE, JAPAN

Sounds so typical, but a baguette with brie and a glass of wine at my Airbnb in Paris overlooking the rooftops.

Buda-best

I love the exquisite food and service at Onyx and Cafe Gerbeaud in Budapest. The atmosphere at Szimpla Kert is second to none! Budapest has the BEST ruin pubs!

Pizza!

MONICA, AUSTRALIA

Ooh, pizza in Naples, Italy. I'll never forget it. The juicy, zingy, fresh juice of tomato dripping on a thin, crispy pizza base, with melting round, white discs of mozzarella and topped with a few basil leaves ... so simple, yet so tasty. It reset my understanding of pizza.

Tea please

ANONYMOUS, IRELAND

Roadside tea shops in Gujarat, India. The true taste of a place is only found when you have a limited budget, open heart and open mind.

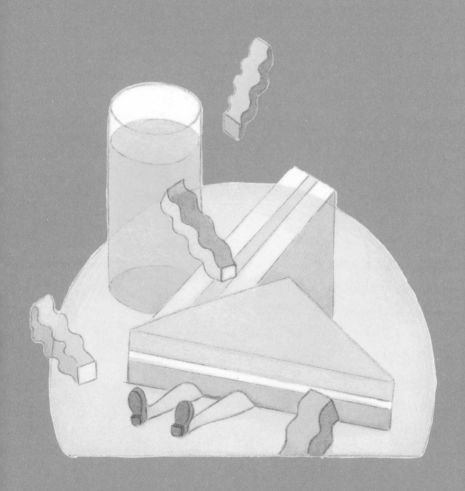

ASIAN GIRLS ARE GOING PLACES

Yellow

The first time I ever visited New York, I landed at midnight, famished, and went straight to the twenty-four-hour diner below my hotel.

I had a very particular craving: I wanted something fatty, to offset my hunger after the flight, and also something fresh, to offset feeling like the walking dead after being trapped in a plane for so long. So I ordered a breakfast juice with a grilled cheese sandwich. Very American. When it arrived, it took me a moment of staring at my meal before I burst out laughing in delirium and horror. The grilled cheese sandwich was yellow, with neon yellow American cheese. It came with a side of fries. Also yellow. The breakfast juice was mostly orange juice, so it too: yellow. The sandwich and fries were served – and I am not making this up – on a yellow plate. It was all being eaten by a yellow person. I have never been more constipated in my life.

Interview with Yumi Stynes

Yumi Stynes is an author and broadcaster, former cook, and total babe. Among her daily responsibilities she presents a radio show on the KIIS Network called *The 3pm Pickup*. She fronts the juggernaut podcast *Ladies, We Need to Talk* on the ABC, which is currently in its fifth season. In 2019 her book *Welcome to Your Period* helped change the conversation around menstruation and her latest book, *Welcome to Consent,* is a bestseller.

ML　　What is your cultural background, and what role does food play in connecting you to your heritage?

YS　　My cultural background is Japanese, so any time I experience Japanese food, I feel like I'm casting a line back through space and history to my own ancestors. It's a strong sensation. Japan has a very proud and extensive food culture – it's not just about what you eat, but the way you eat it, the reverence you show to even the humblest bowl of rice, the ceremony you add. It can be from the littlest things like the way you set your chopsticks down at the completion of your meal. When I was shooting food pictures for my cookbooks, the photographer (an Asian woman) and I would sometimes be aghast at what the (white) food stylist did with the chopsticks. And I don't think we ever explained ourselves well but to this day any time I see professional food photos that include chopsticks I can tell if an Asian person had a say.

ML　　Where does your interest in food come from?

YS　　I always assume *everyone* has the same level of passion about food, but then I eat something terrible and am reminded that this is not true! Food is a lot like sex – it's sensual and daily and fun, but there are a lot of people who are very perfunctory about it!

I used to play this game called 'Fantasy Breakfast'. This is where you wake up with your lover and as you cuddle, you talk about all the delicious things you would like to eat that day. My fantasies would be very detailed and specific and sometimes go on and on. What I discovered was that if I wanted my fantasies to be realised *exactly*, I would often have to make them myself.

When I was a student I worked to support myself in a few kitchen jobs – dishwashing and doing food prep and eventually cooking. So I liked cooking because I was good at it. But I was good at it because I could see from a young age that being able to cook is a very important life skill if you care about what you put in your mouth!

ML   **Where are your favourite places to eat in the world? What are you eating once you get there?**

YS   Just like they say we're in the 'Golden Age of Television', I think Australia is experiencing a Golden Age of Dining. There are so many producers, creators and cooks doing wonderful things in Australia. There's a real pride in artisan products like cheese, bread, oils – and then combine that with the fact that Australia has incredible primary produce like fruit, veg and seafood – and finally add to the mix the chefs who herald from all over the world, particularly Asia, and you can find truly excellent food.

I love to eat anywhere in Melbourne – the basic standard of food is higher than in Sydney. My mum and I always eat at Ocha Restaurant in Kew. It's reliably excellent Japanese, which is what bougie bitches like us count on. I also love going out to regional areas like the Blue Mountains in NSW. There's a vegan restaurant called Secret Creek Cafe which has wallabies hopping around outside and inside there is a brilliant, dedicated chef called Tenille Evans whipping up storms of extraordinary vegan alchemy.

ML   **Where is the best street food?**

YS   Bangkok has the best street food. There is a proper street food culture there! It's lively, cheap, and fresh, and eating it makes you feel like you're participating – doing what locals do. I have lived on beef char kway teow as a backpacker. Nowadays it's more about exotic mango desserts, choosing live seafood and hunting down fresh-squeezed pomegranate juice. During one of my pregnancies I was in Bangkok and would send my partner out looking for the various street foods I had cravings for: usually banana wrapped in sticky rice which then is grilled in banana leaf. The stalls would relocate to different spots in the city each day so you couldn't rely on them being in the same place. He would hunt them down with the dogged determination of a soon-to-be father.

ML   **Do you cook while you're travelling? And if so, what are you making?**

YS   I really miss being able to cook if I'm away for a long time, so if there's an opportunity to cook, I take it! I love cooking for friends so if I'm visiting mates I'll do a cook-up. When I went to Chile I did a cooking class and learnt to make empanadas and a simple sauce called 'pebre'. It's like a salsa and making it involved grating a tomato, finely chopping a white onion, chopping in a good amount of washed coriander, salt and vegetable oil (not olive! The teacher was very insistent!). IT WAS DELICIOUS and I kept making it as a standby – easy to do in a hotel room and delicious on bread. In the cooking class you bite a corner off the empanada then spoon the pebre into the hole. Far out, my mouth is watering just thinking about it.

ML **What is your favourite food memory from your travels?**

YS I like to plan ahead and book at least one fancy restaurant meal per city we visit. When I took my teenage daughters to Bilbao in Spain to go to a music festival, we stopped on the way in Biarritz and San Sebastian. In Biarritz the girls nearly cried for missing their Japanese grandma while we ate fancy seafood and worshipped the view. It was ridiculous and my mum would've loved it. I'm serious – she would've dropped dead from loving it so much! It's lucky we didn't take her! *weepy tears* In San Sebastian the three of us went to an acclaimed restaurant, Arzak, and the solemnity of the setting and our own hyper-expectations made us really keyed up and we got a hectic case of the giggles and we laughed so hard there were tears. Tears and snot! The food was brilliant and the service wonderful but the best part of the memory was from being with my loved ones and feeling so special, so lucky.

ML   What's your favourite thing to browse when you're in the grocery store in a foreign country?

YS   Chips! I am a massive fan of potato chips, crisps, corn puffs, etc. I even have an Instagram where I review chips (@zerofuckscooking) and give them a rating. It's by far the most popular thing I do on social media, people lose their shit for it. But I love a foreign grocery store and could roam the aisles for hours. I'm always on the lookout for something I've never seen before – particularly if it's fresh and grown nearby.

ML   What is the dish you cook to impress your Asian relatives?

YS   Okay. My Asian relatives are VERY HARD TO IMPRESS. One time I took them to the best soba noodle restaurant in Sydney. It was quite a drive away and parking is impossible and to me the whole thing was a big deal and at the end I said, 'What did you think?' And they said, 'It was okay.' So I would not waste my time trying to impress them with something they can have done better at home in Japan. I would cook them something that starts with a killer ingredient – mud crab, in my opinion, is the single greatest seafood there is. Failing that, South Australian rock lobster or really fresh oysters. Asian people LOOOOOVE seafood. (For instance, I have taken my mum to the famous aquarium in Melbourne and she walked around the various exhibits saying, 'Oooh, yum!') The other thing I can do to impress Asian relatives is baking. Japanese households tend to have a stove but no oven, so baking is not really a thing over there.

ML   What is the best food to pack when you're on the go, e.g., flying, on a road trip, bushwalking, etc.?

YS   In every kind of travel you undertake, the easiest food to obtain is processed, packet foods. So you shouldn't pack that. The food that you want to pack is food that you can't get at an airport or service station. When I'm flying, I always pack fresh, raw vegetables like cucumbers and celery, mandarins, apples. It feels like punishment when you're packing it but when you're EATING IT, surrounded by highly processed garbage food, you're always really thankful you thought of it!

I had a brilliant time planning the menu for an eight-day bushwalk where you had to pack every meal and cook everything on a single, tiny stove. A lot of fellow campers were eating dehydrated meals where you add boiling water to a bag, seal it, wait ten minutes and voila! You have 'spaghetti bolognese'! It was gross and they all looked constipated after two days. We were frying fragrant garlic and grating truffled manchego over our pasta and relishing food in the outdoors. We were boiling up dashi broth and dipping buckwheat noodles. Camping and bushwalking is no excuse to eat poorly.

ML   **What is the most fail-safe, crowd-pleasing snack for when you're travelling with kids?**

YS   Good quality, proper Japanese osembei (rice crackers) and nori seaweed. Both snacks aren't nauseating and you can pig out on them without feeling miserable!

ML   **What is the most horrific rendering of an Asian dish you've seen in your life?**

YS   Most of the cheap sushi I see for sale in takeaway places is pretty horrific. It smells bad. My kids regularly eat at a sushi train that is so bad I can't bring myself to sit down in there. They eat and I stand behind them, wishing to die. I remember seeing a friend making miso soup and adding nori seaweed instead of wakame seaweed and noting my look of horror they said, 'It's actually really good!' And I said, 'No it's not.'

ML   What's your go-to fix for when you're sick (spewing, the runs) from a dodgy dish?

YS   When your appetite returns and you're feeling brave enough to face food, I highly recommend a very simple and light dish of natto (fermented soy beans) on hot rice with seaweed. The natto has gut-healing properties and is very gentle and easy to digest. Plus, it weirdly makes you feel powered up and tingly and terrific! It's a challenging food if you've never tried it before but getting past the texture is well worth it.

ML   What would be your last meal on earth?

YS   A crusty white baguette with cold, salted butter and a big mug of strong, hot tea.

ML   Do you have any top tips or general advice when it comes to the intersection of travel and food?

YS   It's always worth asking, 'What do YOU recommend?' when talking to a local – waitstaff, a friend or a street vendor. Most people are really proud to introduce you to something they think is terrific. Seeking out a recommended market, restaurant or food van is a great excuse for getting out and about. It gives your travel purpose!

MEMORABLE

Seeing the light

ANONYMOUS, IRELAND

Seeing the aurora borealis. Being a scientist, I understand why the phenomena occurs. Just the thought that a thin layer of air keeps us from being fried by the sun's radiation and the collision of the intense radiation with our atmosphere creates paintings in neon that are alive and ever-changing ...

MOMENTS

Levelling up
MONICA, AUSTRALIA

There's nothing more exhilarating than realising your foreign language skill has reached that point that you can finally have a truly deep and meaningful conversation with the locals. That is when you know you will have a relationship with that country forever.

Testing times
MEG, SOUTH KOREA

My grossest travel experience is clinging to the walls for dear life on a three-hour train ride from Jakarta to Bandung, having explosive diarrhea into a very wet stainless-steel squat toilet I wasn't flexible enough to use properly. Good times.

WORK AND

PRIVILEGE

Before COVID, I was the type of person who travelled at least twice a month for work. It was exciting to always be in new environments and meeting new people, but eventually I grew tired of it.

I resented the sustained jetlag, the lining up at airport gates, the unpacking and re-packing of bags, and the feeling of never knowing where in the world I was – quite literally. I wanted nothing more than to stay at home, nest, and while away the hours doing nothing in my room. (Boy, did the COVID-19 pandemic show me!) I'm embarrassed to admit that it took the shutting down of my home country and the wider world to show me just how incredibly lucky and privileged I was to be travelling regularly to begin with. Now I swear on the travel gods that I will never take that ability for granted again!

Work

Regardless of the sphere in which you work (this includes the domestic sphere – being a stay-at-home mother deserves the same respect and benefits of any other job because being a parent is *more* than a full-time job!) there will come a time when your working life and travel will intersect. And whether it's travelling for meetings and conferences, or navigating new workplace cultures in different countries, Asian women are uniquely placed professionally. We must navigate both sexism and racism while doing our jobs brilliantly. And we're expected to do all of that while looking polished at all times, without ever tripping up. It's a lot of pressure – and a kind of pressure we should not be subjected to – but if anyone can handle that pressure, it's Asian women. I mean, think of your schooling days. If there's anything I've learnt from studying non-stop for twelve hours surrounded by empty Shin Ramen cups with Cantopop blasting in the background, it's resilience.

Yellow fever in the USA

I've had my fair share of uncomfortable experiences with non-Asian men – particularly older, white men – who exoticise and sexualise me because of my ethnicity.

There have been instances at work where I'm the token Asian woman in the room, which has meant having to navigate outright or more insidious displays of fetishisation by white colleagues. It doesn't matter where in the world I might be working; it's always a delicate balancing act of wanting to keep my job while wanting to call things out and hold people to account, which can be annoying at best and straight up dangerous at worst.

One of the most unsettling instances of this exoticisation happened on a month-long work trip I took to Chicago. There were around twenty people in my program, from diverse age groups, races, and genders. There was also one notably older, white man (let's call him Lester), which would not have been an issue if ... he would just stop staring at me. During classes, I would feel Lester's gaze on me and so with every team exercise, I would make a concerted effort to avoid him physically. During lunch breaks, Lester would make lewd, sexist jokes with either me or my classmates, referring to the 'girlfriends I have in every Asian country'. Everyone else (the teacher and participants, none of whom were Asian themselves) would laugh and say, 'Oh that's so typical of him. He's such a creep!' But I couldn't laugh it off; he made me deeply uncomfortable and when he learnt of my discomfort, he doubled down and went to even greater lengths to make me feel uneasy.

When I expressed my discomfort to my male classmates, they gaslit me, telling me that Lester was like that with all women (like somehow this made his behaviour more acceptable?) and I found myself drifting away from them too; if they were willing to let his behaviour fly, I didn't want to associate with them either. When the workshop finally ended, we all exchanged business cards. Unsurprisingly, Lester's business card featured a photoshopped picture of himself looking much younger, with Chinese characters typed on the back. I felt ill and threw the card in the bin. I made a complaint in the feedback form for the workshop and never went back to the organisation. Years later, the CEO of the organisation stepped down amid allegations of institutionalised racism. I do not wish the organisation or Lester well.

He made me deeply uncomfortable and when he learnt of my discomfort, he doubled down

Interview with Bhakthi Puvanenthiran

Bhakthi Puvanenthiran is editor of *ABC Everyday*. Previously, she was managing editor of Crikey, covering politics and the media, as well as a journalist and editor at *The Age* and *The Sydney Morning Herald*, reporting on arts, entertainment, and business. Bhakthi is currently a judge of the Walkley Awards for Journalism and a regular media commentator.

ML   What is your cultural background and how has it influenced your relationship to work?

BP   My family and I are Eelam Tamils and we come from the northern part of Sri Lanka, a predominantly Tamil town named Jaffna. There are a few parts to it [the relationship between my background and my relationship with work] – firstly like many, many migrants my family moved to Australia to ensure that we were educated well and got good jobs so that has always been a priority. I went to a bluestone university and have always focused on paid work in senior roles in my industry as a result of that expectation. But there is more to the story: as a teen I wanted to become a journalist out of my concern for the lack of freedom of speech that many Tamils experienced during the civil war and continue to face.

ML   You lead a team at work. Are there times when being an Asian woman informs the way you lead, manage staff, and approach professional challenges – e.g., being more collective-minded, delegating, etc.?

BP   I definitely have a more 'let's figure this out together and listen to each other' approach, from editing someone's writing through to leading a team through difficult changes. Part of it is definitely cultural; where I come from, how you act is primarily judged on how it affects the people around you, and so that kind of selfish, macho, individualistic leadership style has never worked for me and frankly I'm not entirely sure it works as well as people think it does. I'm also really conscious of cultural differences, or I try to be, with the team. When I see someone from a non-Anglo background not putting themselves forward I do ask them the question again and get them to reconsider whether they are just being polite. We don't just exist to serve others as we may have been raised to think.

ML   **What are some challenges you've faced in your industry as an Asian woman?**

BP   It's tricky to know what challenges exist for everyone else and therefore how my identity has played into those issues. I chose to work in an industry which is by and large in financial decline, so then I guess all the challenges of finding work and doing the work you really want feels heightened. I definitely didn't have any obvious role models for the career I wanted so it was difficult to know where I fit in. I also have been told that I am too 'soft' to be a hard news reporter or a leader, which I reject because my style is very collective-oriented and I think that comes from the way I was raised. It's a highly respectful culture.

ML   Do you have any female, Asian role models you look up to in your field? (Or even outside of the field?)

BP   There are a few. Leadership I would say Leah Jing McIntosh, founder of Liminal magazine, Andrea Ho who is now at the Judith Nielsen Institute and Que Minh Luu of Netflix. In terms of writing Michelle de Kretser, Arundhati Roy, and Brami Jegan.

ML   Before the coronavirus, how much did you travel for work?

BP   In my current role I was probably travelling every other month, mostly interstate.

ML   What essentials do you pack for a work trip?

BP   Joan Didion famously had a very cool packing list for her journalism assignments which was like one black sweater, one lace bra and a notebook. I can assure you my regular packing list is more like: phone charger, Ventolin and audiobook. For work I carry a laptop, tablet and big fat desk diary everywhere because I hate my back. My main form of exercise is *Yoga with Adriene* and walking, and you can do both of those absolutely anywhere so I do try and keep up while I'm away and take some stretchy pants and a t-shirt to make it happen. I'm also very fussy about skincare and only use body oils so I always take those but in a separate plastic ziplock bag to avoid spills.

ML Travelling can throw a spanner in your routine. How do you stay fresh and look professional when you're on the road?

BP I wear an 'official Melbourne girl' black linen dress and white sneakers on the plane but always have some lovely perfume oil with me. Another hot tip is having big gold earrings that can go with anything and a Nars lip pencil. Suddenly very ready to see people.

ML How do you stay focused on work when there are so many distractions when you're travelling? (So many cool things to see! So many delicious things to eat!)

BP My main distraction when I'm travelling for work is that I want to socialise with everyone I know in a city while I'm there and then I wear myself out and am too tired for work, so now I try and stagger it so I'm only seeing people every other night and I have rest nights where I'm just in bed by 9pm.

ML Is there a work tool (e.g., an app, notebook, software) that you can't live without when you're travelling?

BP The weather app. No better satisfaction than packing perfectly for the climate you're going to.

No better
satisfaction than
packing perfectly
for the climate
you're going to

Privilege

If you are reading this book you likely have a certain level of privilege, specifically the privilege of wealth (in order to afford said book) and access to education (in order to read said book).

Travelling is a rich person's game. After all, the very concept of modern travel as we know it – travel for self-actualisation – has its roots in the Grand Tours undertaken by aristocratic young Europeans of the 17th and 18th centuries. And while it makes me feel ill when I see white travellers in developing countries begging for money to fund the next stage of their trips, I do recognise that I myself am extremely privileged, especially when it comes to my ethnicity and class. I come from a middle-class Chinese family that benefits from the relative poverty of, and intercultural racism directed at, other groups of Asian people. (There is, undeniably, a racist hierarchy among East and South Asian ethnicity groups. Is there any wonder why skin-bleaching creams and treatments are so prevalent, and fairness is considered the pinnacle of 'beauty'?) So how can we, as Asian women from different backgrounds, navigate the politics of ethnicity and class? How can we travel in ways that are ethically sound? And how can we explore the world in good conscience when it has been irrevocably damaged by climate change?

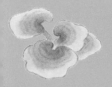

How to
not be a jerk to locals

Tourism can make or break an economy, but this can feel like a double-edged sword when you're considered wealthy in relation to the locals. It's easy to be an exploitative, bourgeois foreigner, but there are small and tangible ways in which you can make your travel more ethical and beneficial to local communities.

Tip top

Tip generously if you are in a position to do so.

Beggar beliefs

Whether or not you choose to give money to beggars comes down to your own beliefs, but I tend to give as much as I can because, whatever that person's situation may be, they are still doing it tougher than I am. (My mother has told me that I'm naïve as 'beggar gangs' can sometimes be run by crime rings, but I refuse to believe every beggar is a victim of a beggar gang.)

The clothes off your back

English actress Helen Mirren once said in an interview that she only travels with underwear and the clothes on her back. Once she arrives at her destination, she buys all of her clothes for that trip from a charity store and then donates the clothing back once she leaves. This injects money back into the community.

Ask before snapping

Ask permission before taking photos of someone. Some cultures have superstitions about photographs, but beyond that, it's just general courtesy.

Custom-ise

Have an understanding of local customs and follow them. And learn some of the language. Even if it's incredibly sloppy, locals will appreciate that you've gone to the effort instead of assuming that everyone speaks a dominant language like English or Mandarin.

Do your homework

Don't fall for voluntourism – do your research and make sure you're working with organisations that truly benefit the people you have gone to 'help'. Some dodgy organisations direct money to the company directors, while others are built on making the experience fulfilling and comfortable for the volunteers themselves – helping them 'grow' as individuals, rather than directing that funding towards community development that addresses systemic issues. On this note – buy directly from local and indigenous artisans so you know where your money is going. Non-indigenous people and conglomerates can sometimes exploit and profit off these practitioners.

I definitely feel that if I'm travelling at all it's from a position of privilege, by virtue of me being able to do it. This was particularly obvious everywhere we went in Indonesia, with AUD in our pockets, and just felt kinda shitty a lot of the time. For example, for an orangutan hike, we'd hired a guide to take just us around (which was insane in itself). He was super helpful, and super hardworking, and hadn't really charged us much, so at the end I think we gave him the equivalent of maybe an extra AU$50. He was gobsmacked, and thought it was a mistake at first, then was just incredibly, incredibly thankful and a bit emotional. It was kind of upsetting that just because of the value of our currency we, a couple half his age, could elicit that kind of response just by giving him the equivalent of about two hours of casual work back in Australia.

Meg, South Korea

How to not be a jerk to the environment

Here's the deal: the planet is warming at an unprecedented rate and human beings are to blame. Ecosystems are dying; animals are becoming endangered or extinct due to the destruction of their habitats; and island nations and coastal cities will eventually either disappear or be damaged by rising sea levels. Not only that (!) – did you know that each week humans ingest enough microplastics from tainted food and water to make a credit card? Yech. But don't despair! There are still things we can all do to help negate some of the effects of climate change, even while travelling.

Try ...

1

Making use of public transport and walking as much as you can.

2

Carrying your own reusable water bottle, cutlery and grocery bags with you.

3

Leaving your destination as you found it. Take your rubbish with you until you find a receptacle where you can dispose of it.

4

Packing light to reduce carbon emissions, e.g., pack an e-reader over physical books.

5

Flying as little as possible, but if you must, pay for the carbon offset. And choose direct flights as take-offs and landings use the most fuel.

6

If you're driving, rent hybrid or electric cars.

7

Choosing accommodation with eco-friendly approaches. While you're there, use the same towel rather than requesting they be refreshed each day. And if the place isn't a pigsty, leave the 'Do Not Disturb' sign on the door to reduce the chemicals and electricity used by cleaners. Switch off lights when you're not in the room and choose showers over baths. And of course: recycle! If there is no way to recycle, encourage your accommodation to implement a recycling system on a comment card.

8

Bringing your own amenities. Bars of soap use less plastic than gel packaging, and the travel toiletries in hotels can instead be taken and donated to crisis accommodation centres.

10

Using period underwear, reusable pads, or cups to cut back on sanitary items. It takes 500 to 800 years for sanitary pads to decompose.

9

If you're hiking, stay on marked trails. Trails are demarcated to ensure endangered flora and fauna aren't trampled on. And speaking of wildlife, avoid engaging in animal tourism where animals are drugged or abused. If not to protect the native wildlife, do it to avoid looking like a straight white man on a dating app.

11

Eating less meat, or no meat at all. (The aforementioned buffets in the 'Culture and Food' chapter may be an exception ... ahem.) Animal farming is responsible for an enormous amount of carbon emissions. But this is good advice generally if you're travelling to a country you've never been to before and your digestive system is adjusting to the local fare.

Travel toiletries in hotels can instead be taken and donated to crisis accommodation centres

FINAL

TIPS

Okay: so you've booked everything and you're ready to go. So why are you still reading this book? And why do you have a niggling feeling that you've forgotten something?

I'll tell you why. Because you have forgotten something! And because I'm here to tell you what you've forgotten in this chapter before you can take off/set sail/drive away! And because like any Asian family talking in a restaurant and then talking in the restaurant carpark and then stopping at traffic lights to talk to each other through open car windows, I am terrible at goodbyes! So enjoy this final chapter, fellow traveller. I hope it fills you with excitement, last-minute practical advice and preparedness for your next adventure.

Packing!

— Roll your clothes! Rolling is a lot more space saving than folding and ensures your clothes aren't as crinkled when you unpack. Who wants to iron while they're travelling? No one. And who wants to waste money paying someone else to iron their clothes? I'd rather die.

— Invest in a good-quality toiletry bag with a hook so it can be hung. These normally have compartments that make it easier to find smaller items and prevent finicky things like necklaces and cords getting tangled.

— Have both physical and electronic copies of important documents in case of emergencies. And split cash between different wallets in case your luggage is stolen or goes missing. (I can hear my mother's voice here: 'Don't think you can trust airport staff!')

— Pack a handheld scale to weigh your luggage to prevent any surprise fees at the airport. See above re: wasting money. I repeat: I'd rather die than pay extra for anything.

Essentials

Regardless of where I'm travelling, I always have the following handy:

- spare change in the correct currency (for public transport, vending machines, or to use a restroom charging a fee)

- electrolyte drinks, tablets, or powders (in case I become ill and dehydrated)

- pocket tissues (in case there is no toilet paper in public restrooms)

- a plastic bag (for rubbish when I'm on the go, or, let's face it – when there's a bathroom emergency).

Money

Have a daily budget

Have a daily budget, and avoid using credit cards. I like to use a rechargeable travel card to keep track of spending because I have absolutely no self control. (Especially when it comes to books, and those things are heavy. Which then leads to ... you guessed it – extra luggage fees.)

Travel during the off season

Travel during the off season and choose destinations where your home currency will take you further.

Choose hostels and Airbnbs

Choose hostels and Airbnbs over hotels, and consider subletting your own home while you're away. This is doubly useful if you have pets that need minding.

Keep all your receipts

If you're travelling for work, keep all your receipts for tax time, and buy business insurance for income protection/in case any electronics get damaged.

Buy a local SIM

If your phone is not locked to a provider, buy a SIM locally. Or better yet – buy a SIM online beforehand and switch it over in the plane as you're landing so you're always connected. (This is my favourite and most-used hack because it's also linked to safety – when you've got a SIM ready you're always in touch with someone, no matter where you are in the world.)

Mindful gifting

Globalisation makes buying truly special souvenirs a difficult task. I learnt this the hard way when I stocked up on Japanese snacks at a 100 yen store, only to arrive home to discover the same snacks at my local grocer. Sigh. Choose gifts that take up little space and are specific to the region in which you're travelling, like key rings, crafts or magnets with a local twist.

Make the most of the buffet

If you're staying somewhere with a breakfast buffet, channel your inner Asian mother and fill some napkins with pastries. And take whole fruit with peels (nature's packaging!) like bananas and oranges with you for your bag. (Cut fruit can very quickly be exposed to bacteria.)

Lunch over dinner

Eat a big and fancy lunch, instead of a big and fancy dinner. Lunch is often slightly cheaper than dinner and restaurants are less busy during the day.

Stock up at the local supermarket

Stock up at the local supermarket or convenience store and never, EVER take from the mini bar! (If you've ever been haunted by your ancestors, it's because of that one time you took a ten-dollar bar of chocolate from the mini bar. Unforgivable.)

Avoid eating at tourist sites

And last but not least: avoid eating around expensive tourist areas. Actually, avoid eating in areas packed with tourists, generally. Ask the locals where they eat and you'll likely get a better deal as well as a better meal.

Acknowledgements

A big thank you to the team at Hardie Grant – Melissa Kayser and Megan Cuthbert – for bringing this travel guide series to life, and my endless gratitude to my editor Allison Hiew; it means so much to have worked with and be guided by the genius of another Asian woman. Thank you for making me sound smarter and more articulate than I actually am!

Thank you to the best agents in the biz, Jennifer Naughton and Candice Thom, for their endless support and cat memes.

Thank you to all of the brilliant women I surveyed, whose wise words appear in the pages of this book. I'm so incredibly grateful for you taking the time out of your busy lives to chat to me.

And last but not least, thank you to my mother, Jenny Phang Puen Chun, and my two grandmothers, See Sam Looi and Wong Law Ching Lan, who are both watching over me. You are the original explorers in our family and without you and the sacrifices you made throughout your lives, I could not be writing these words today.

About the author

Michelle Law 羅敏儀 is an award-winning writer and actor based in the Eora Nation (Sydney, Australia).

She began her career in the literary world, writing fiction, essays and journalism.

Nowadays, she mostly writes for theatre and television.

Her most recent works include the plays *Single Asian Female* and *Miss Peony*, and the web series *Homecoming Queens*.

In her spare time, she enjoys watching trashy reality shows, buying new stationery, and belting her heart out at karaoke.

You can find out more about Michelle via her website, Twitter or Instagram.

michelle-law.com
@ms_michellelaw
@msmichellelaw

Most of her posts are about her tabby cat, Bean.

Published in 2022 by Hardie Grant Explore,
an imprint of Hardie Grant Publishing

Hardie Grant Explore (Melbourne)
Wurundjeri Country
Building 1, 658 Church Street
Richmond, Victoria 3121

Hardie Grant Explore (Sydney)
Gadigal Country
Level 7, 45 Jones Street
Ultimo, NSW 2007

www.hardiegrant.com/au/explore

NATIONAL
LIBRARY
OF AUSTRALIA

A catalogue record for this
book is available from the
National Library of Australia

Hardie Grant acknowledges the Traditional Owners of the Country
on which we work, the Wurundjeri people of the Kulin Nation and the
Gadigal people of the Eora Nation, and recognises their continuing
connection to the land, waters and culture. We pay our respects to their
Elders past and present.

Asian Girls Are Going Places
ISBN 9781741177121

10 9 8 7 6 5 4 3 2 1

Publisher Melissa Kayser
Project editor Megan Cuthbert
Editor Allison Hiew
Proofreader Leeyong Soo
Design Evi-O.Studio | Evi O & Nicole Ho
Typesetting Hannah Schubert

Printed in Singapore by 1010 Printing International Limited